Voices from the Valley
True Stories from the Hood River Valley

Copyright © 2012 Good Catch Publishing, Beaverton, OR.

All rights reserved. Written permission must be secured from the publisher to use or reproduce any part of this book, except for brief quotations in critical reviews or articles.

This book was written for the express purpose of conveying the love and mercy of Jesus Christ. The statements in this book are substantially true; however, names and minor details have been changed to protect people and situations from accusation or incrimination.

All Scripture quotations, unless otherwise noted, are taken from the New International Version Copyright 1973, 1984, 1987 by International Bible Society.

Published in Beaverton, Oregon, by Good Catch Publishing.
www.goodcatchpublishing.com
V1.1

Printed in the United States of America

Table of Contents

	Acknowledgements	9
	Introduction	13
1	Tasting Triumph	15
2	Safe	39
3	Five Thousand Miles	67
4	Down A Winding Road	95
5	A Wonderful Life	115
6	Healing Words	141
7	Fearless Forgiveness	163
	Conclusion	189

Acknowledgements

I would like to thank Terrell Abbott for his vision for this book and Joy Haystead for her hard work in making it a reality. And to the people of River of Life Assembly, thank you for your boldness and vulnerability in sharing your personal stories.

This book would not have been published without the amazing efforts of our project manager and editor, Jeannette Scott. Her untiring resolve pushed this project forward and turned it into a stunning victory. Thank you for your great fortitude and diligence. Deep thanks to our incredible Editor in Chief, Michelle Cuthrell, and Executive Editor, Jen Genovesi, for all the amazing work they do. I would also like to thank our invaluable proofreader, Melody Davis, for the focus and energy she has put into perfecting our words.

Lastly, I want to extend our gratitude to the creative and very talented Jenny Randle, who designed the beautiful cover for *Voices from the Valley: True Stories from the Hood River Valley.*

Daren Lindley
President and CEO
Good Catch Publishing

The book you are about to read
is a compilation of authentic life stories.
The facts are true, and the events are real.
These storytellers have dealt with crisis, tragedy, abuse
and neglect and have shared their most private moments,
mess-ups and hang-ups in order for others to learn and
grow from them. In order to protect the identities of those
involved in their pasts, the names and details of some
storytellers have been withheld or changed.

Introduction

What do you do when life is careening out of control? When addiction has overtaken you or abuse chained you with fear? Is depression escapable? Will relationships ever be healthy again? Are we destined to dissolve into an abyss of sorrow? Or will the sunlight of happiness ever return?

Your life really can change. It is possible to become a new person. The seven stories you are about to read prove positively that people right here in our town have stopped dying and started living. Whether they've been beaten by abuse, broken promises, shattered dreams or suffocating addictions, the resounding answer is, "Yes! You can become a new person." The potential to break free from gloom and into a bright future awaits.

Expect inspiration, hope and transformation! As you walk with the real people from our very own city through the pages of this book, you will not only find riveting accounts of their hardships; you will learn the secrets that brought about their breakthroughs. These people are no longer living in the shadows of yesterday; they are thriving with a sense of mission and purpose TODAY. May these stories inspire you to do the same.

Tasting Triumph
The Story of Bill Perkins
Written by Richard Drebert

In early spring, we were at war to keep the orchard blossoms alive.

Diesel exhaust stung my eyes, and I shivered next to my father on the iron tractor seat.

Dad downshifted and the Diamond Fruit Growers' crawler growled lower notes, pausing in the orchard row like a team of harnessed oxen. Dad's boots crackled frost when he hopped down to the tilled soil, and he lit diesel fuel inside the burner pan of his last smudge pot. Like an old farmer chuffing a pipe, the crusty pot's 3-foot chimney belched white smoke.

Dad nodded toward his smudge pot army standing guard among hundreds of apple trees. Each burner puffed billows of warmth into the crisp morning air.

"Just a few more days, and I think we got it. Temperatures are on the rise …"

He spoke his sentiments absently into the low-hanging smoke, and I nodded, like it was to me.

I was proud of my father. He was winning his battle to save the Diamond orchards again.

Dad's thoughts flowed like water through a flume, with specific gates at the end of every rill. If you needed to know where his mind was headed, you had to be patient. Deep weather lines from sun and wind etched my father's weary face, and he glanced down the rows of apple trees, blossoming gaily — like they didn't have a care.

Heavy responsibilities were pruning years from my father. In the 1940s, he fought his war on two fronts: against weather and the government. World War II made Dad's job much harder. He needed ration stamps to buy tires for his employer's trucks or steel to repair machinery. Dad required fuel to run a farm of several hundred acres, but the government treated diesel and gasoline like ambrosia, rationing out a few gallons at a time.

My father had that rare quality that demanded respect from the men he hired for the orchard owners and a gift for caring for living things. But he wasn't the only one in the family who carried a wartime burden. My mother stood in line to purchase commodities like sugar and flour — suddenly allotted by ration stamps per members in a family.

Mom and Dad believed it was their duty to join the war against the Nazis, and they gave up more than necessities: They gave their eldest son. Raymond was 10 years older than I. At 18, he marched off to boot camp to learn to fight. I was 8 years old when he left our big old farmhouse — and my mother in tears.

My father was right. Temperatures rose that spring, soothing the apple and pear blossoms. The threat of frost slunk out of the Hood River Valley, and too few letters came from Raymond. Hitler continued to menace the world, and my little brother and I scurried like noisy

Tasting Triumph

squirrels in the orchards, hiding in our own make-believe bunkers. Our missions originated in Mom's kitchen where she baked bread in a wood-burning stove — but my older sister, Iretta, tried to wreck our combat plans. While we flung apples like grenades, she complained that we should be weeding the garden with her.

As a child running wild in the orchards, I had no clue that later in life I would face a foe as deadly as any Panzer unit. I would taste battle in a way that few men do — and come to know peace beyond anything I could imagine.

❧❧❧

I swayed in my bunk with a thousand other soldiers, off the coast of Alaska where the icy green froth whipped the USNS *HB Freeman* — reminding me of Mom beating pancake batter. After weeks aboard the old General (Freeman was a Civil War commander), I understood why the aged transport ship groaned. Every day at 8 a.m., I stood in ragged rows of puking soldiers above deck for mandatory exercise and "fresh" air.

Along the Inside Passage on the way to South Korea, the *Freeman* climbed drunkenly to the top of steep seawater mountains, then crashed down into the water's valleys. Its turbines whinnied for seconds like unbridled work horses while the massive single screw (propeller) spun in thin air.

Then up, up the General climbed, only to freewheel dizzily and drown its bow under water again. Our queasy

17

Voices from the Valley

bellies rode the old bucket to the bottom of each swell, where rivets and welds groaned, lamenting the General's belated retirement.

My Army unit looked forward to a date with duty at Inchon, Korea. I swung deep in thought in a web of stacked Army berths, breathing transport aromas — armpits, cigarette smoke, aftershave and vomit — waiting for the 21 days of tedium to end.

❧❧❧

Mom and Dad had been slaves to the seasons for as long as I could remember: Mom canned garden fare, like beans, cabbage and tomatoes, and Dad butchered pigs and bought salmon from the Klamath Indians, to stock up before hard winters.

Before my high school graduation, Dad had tossed his last pear into a wooden crate and sprayed his last apple tree. He moved us three kids and Mom to the city of Hood River, which anyone from Portland likely called a hick town.

In the cold season between planting and harvest, Dad's paychecks from the Diamond Fruit Growers froze solid like the local ponds. Part of his contract with Diamond had always included our free farmhouse, but the cash for his work stopped from October through February.

It was a wonderful thing when my parents received a steady paycheck throughout the whole calendar year!

Dad landed a plumb job maintaining refrigeration

Tasting Triumph

units at the Diamond packing plant, and I worked there, too — until I got drafted into the Army infantry. The Korea Armistice had been signed in 1953, but South Korea and the United Nations needed U.S. troops to defend their border trenches at the Demilitarized Zone (DMZ). Occasionally, a mortar round still took out a patrol during the uneasy peace.

I adapted well to Army life at Fort Ord, Monterey Bay, California. Hand-to-hand combat, firing bazookas and radio training came as naturally to me as repairing a tractor engine. My M-1 Garand rifle became my constant companion.

At 20 years old, I felt confident in my future and glad to see Hood River from my rearview mirror. Like an Army pack strapped too tight, my religious heritage had begun to chafe me, growing more and more uncomfortable. Back home we *never* missed a Sunday or Wednesday service at the Assemblies of God church my aunts, uncles and cousins attended, too. Our church was one of thousands of tiny Pentecostal congregations birthed from the Azusa Street Revival of 1906 that swept through the Western, Southeastern and Midwestern states.

A dynamic "new" Pentecostal creed percolated in nearly every evangelical denomination in the country — lively preachers said that Jesus was still alive and *present*. He still healed the sick. He still delivered drunks from their poison. He forgave the most horrendous sins. Men and women preachers taught that his powerful Spirit would inhabit the soul of anyone who humbly asked. Dad had encountered this Jesus in Arkansas; my mom and her family, in Oklahoma. They left Oklahoma in 1929, during the Dust Bowl drought, and replanted strong seeds of faith in the fertile soil at Hood River. Other family members followed, adding a true Okie Pentecostal flavor to our congregation of about 60 people.

I grew up a church kid, accepting Jesus at Mom's leading, attending youth gatherings and playing trumpet in our church's band. But somewhere in my teens I had decided to stow away religion like a handy wrench that I figured I'd never need.

☙☙☙

At the port in South Korea, I climbed down the heavy rope webbing to landing craft idling on the starboard side of the *Freeman*, and our transports hauled us over the mudflats to Inchon.

We stripped off our stateside duds and layered up wool garments and heavier socks for our pack boots. It was a winter to remember.

The Army assigned me as a 57mm recoilless rifle gunner, and I was the spittin' image of my dad when he was my age: dark hair, wiry and 135 pounds. By the time I got my field pack strapped on *and* shouldered the 5-foot-long, 40-pound anti-tank gun, I looked like an overloaded pony.

Mercifully, I landed back in my old rifle squad, and the captain put me in charge of the communications for our

Tasting Triumph

infantry company. I spent 21 months and six days in the U.S. Army before I was honorably discharged as a corporal.

☙☙☙

When a young man comes home after his military hitch, he feels a little like a Thanksgiving turkey: fresh-cooked and on the dinner table, everyone's eyes glued upon him. When I lit up a cigarette, Mom knew it. If I had a few drinks with the boys, Dad was bound to drive by. Uncles, aunts, cousins and friends all had my best interest at heart, but I just kept drifting toward whatever I hoped might fill an emptiness in my heart.

None of my attractive friends lived a meaningful life, nor did I. Over the next five years, I dated several girls, all of whom fell short of my ideal of a woman. And Mom's prayers must have hit the mark, too, because I never married any that I dated.

I look back now and see that God protected me from making a life-long blunder. I would have been utterly miserable without Claudia — the little girl in a bright green raincoat.

☙☙☙

"Well, hello there, Bill Perkins."

I was on the way to snag the best seats at a football game when a stunning girl who looked real familiar smiled at me. Suddenly, the seats could wait.

Voices from the Valley

"Hey, I know you. Your daddy delivers wood, right? And you used to ride along with him. I remember … you wore a green coat …"

The young woman rolled her eyes. "I was only 8 years old *then*."

Claudia had certainly grown up … but I didn't say what I was thinking.

In the weeks to come, I rerouted my life so that I could get to know this intriguing college girl. Claudia captivated me. I was drawn to her faith, compassion, steadiness, cheerfulness, *peace*. When I asked if she might find time in her busy schedule for a dinner out, she said, "Bill, you'll have to ask my mother."

I beat down butterflies, practiced my most respectful voice and made her mom's acquaintance.

I discovered that Claudia's father was ill with stomach cancer, and I dated Claudia during this difficult year of her life before he passed away. It was a privilege to grieve the loss of her dad with her and her mother.

In 1962, I asked Claudia to marry me, and our community celebrated the joining of two respected Hood River families.

❦❦❦

Claudia and I married while I worked at Neal Creek Lumber Company. We had two wonderful daughters, Megan and Dena, two years apart, and Claudia ran our household and worked a job sometimes, too, to help make

Tasting Triumph

ends meet. Early in our marriage, Claudia's faith showed brightly like snow on Mt. Hood — it never left my view. Each week she and my girls dressed in their Sunday best to attend the liturgical church that Claudia had grown up in, while I busied myself with yard work or invented other duties that "couldn't wait."

My family settled me, completed me, but I still held fast to old habits that troubled Claudia — and me, too, when I was honest with myself. I drank beer with my friends. When I stumbled into the house on Saturday night smelling like a smudge pot, Claudia ironed my shirt and slacks just in case …

"Come to church with me, Bill."

She never meant to shame me. But on Sunday mornings, I felt like a sullen 8 year old after a whipping. (One time Jerry and I had raided Mom's chicken coop for hen's eggs and pitched a cool dozen against an old oak tree. So much fun! Until Dad rounded up the cow near the oak.) Claudia's gentle, loving persuasion always felt like an apple sapling applied to my rear end.

I had attended her church, a very orthodox meeting hall filled with well-dressed and proper folk. It felt stifling, and it rankled me that she thought I needed church at all. I had an answer that usually took the sting out of welts on my conscience.

"Why should I go to the church where my drinking buddies go? God hasn't changed them one bit!"

Claudia couldn't answer that one. She just hooked the hanger with my Sunday suit over the door as she left the house with the girls. When she came home, she quietly hung my suit in the closet again before making lunch.

Claudia grew close to my mother over the years. She spent hours in the kitchen where she confided in Mom. Together they baptized jars of fruit in boiling water. Something unnerving took place in my mom's kitchen, because Claudia always came home with a smile sweeter than pear sauce.

One day Claudia mentioned to her very formal pastor that Jesus could do miracles if she had faith. Claudia was convinced that Jesus was the same "yesterday, today and forever," like the Bible said. Her pastor just laughed at her, and Claudia decided to find people who believed in Jesus the way she did.

Her search led her to the Assemblies of God church that my folks had attended since the 1930s.

Ten years before my mother and father moved to Hood River, a serious freeze had changed the community forever. A cold front slammed our valley with temperatures dipping to 27 degrees below zero. The heavy frost destroyed the apple crops.

To offset future weather-related losses, growers had planted hundreds of cold-resistant pear trees in their orchards and over the years built a multimillion-dollar industry. Now Hood River leads the world in producing sweet Anjou pears.

Like these pioneer orchardists in Hood River, my wife wisely planned ahead, too. She replanted her unwavering

Tasting Triumph

faith with like-minded, godly folks to help her family endure the harshest seasons.

For more than 10 years, I had been employed by several Hood River companies, and the last one, Mayflower Milk, laid me off. I took a temporary part-time job with a beer and wine distributor and moonlighted at whatever I could find.

When Pastor Gamlen, from Claudia's Pentecostal church, started pestering me every Wednesday (my day off), I paused in my projects long enough to offer a lemonade just to be polite. The pastor never seemed put off by my attitude — even when I got down to brass tacks about what I figured he was after.

"Reverend, I got two kids, a wife and a house payment. I work two or three jobs. I know you have a building program going on — but I just don't have extra money to give."

Pastor Gamlen smiled, shaking his head. "Bill, don't you worry about it. I'd just like to see you in church sometime."

I figured he still wanted something, so I relented. "Tell you what I'll do," I said, "I'll help you work on the building some time."

Pastor Gamlen's face lit up, like he hooked a steelhead. "We'd appreciate that, Bill."

The next Saturday, he called.

I got to know the men who sheet-rocked and painted the new building, and they weren't so straight-laced as I'd thought. In fact, I could see myself actually liking some of them, and the next time Claudia hung my suit coat on the door, I put it on.

On a hot summer morning in 1972, I sat in the very back of the Assemblies of God church on a hard pew, shifting, crossing one leg, then the other — and shifting again. I kept asking myself, *What in the world am I doing here?* until Pastor Gamlen must have read my mind.

"Somebody's here this morning, and you're wondering why. It's because God wants you in church today."

He droned on and on, while I sweated and squirmed.

When I closed my eyes, I could see a little boy kneeling with his mother, asking Jesus to be his Savior — and I knew it was me.

My heart felt like it was going to beat out of my chest, and I felt so *heavy*, like I carried that 57mm anti-tank gun again.

My uncle, Mom's older brother, sat in the pew in front of me. His head and shoulders hid me pretty well from the preacher. Suddenly he turned around and fixed me with eyes that looked just like Mom's.

"Son, come on. If you'll go up to the altar, I'll go with ya."

I stood up and followed my uncle to the front of the church, where Pastor Gamlen waited.

My daughters, then ages 6 and 4, watched their daddy kneel down and tell Jesus that he was truly sorry for going his own way for so many years.

The moment that I gave my life to God, I looked around to see who lifted that cumbersome anti-tank gun

Tasting Triumph

off my back. I felt scrubbed clean inside. Free! Utter relief swept over me.

My bills hadn't evaporated into thin air. My job prospects were still in doubt. I had habits that I needed to change. I had a lot to learn about being a good father and husband — but I experienced a peace that I couldn't explain to anyone. I knew that everything was going to be okay, now that I served Jesus.

At home after service that evening, I sat in my girls' playground swing, cogitating on my new commitment to Jesus and fighting off the urge to light up a cancer stick.

"Lord, if I'm going to really live this Christian life, I have to get rid of this habit. But I can't do it by myself."

My lust for cigarettes gradually dissolved like the morning mist on the Hood River, and I haven't smoked a cigarette since.

I felt convinced I shouldn't be working to supply stores with a product that dulled the senses to right and wrong and asked my boss to look for a replacement so I could stop driving the beer and wine route.

My older brother, Raymond, had come back from war unwilling to go to church. He worked as a salesman, and our paths crossed often during the day while I was on the beer runs. Ray noticed right away that there was something different about me.

"Did you quit smokin'?" He stared at my front pocket, never without a pack of coffin nails, and frowned.

"I gotta talk to you, Ray," I said and described my experience with God. The tears in his eyes spoke clearly about the yearning he felt in his heart. Years later, he gave his life to Jesus, too.

※ ※ ※

My cousin bought out the beer distribution company, and I could have trucked booze all over the county, squirreling away a pretty good union wage over the years. But I chose a more profitable route.

"Good morning, Mr. Perkins! Got my Bible with me! See?" A little girl dragging her brother up the church bus steps waved a tattered Bible at me. I grinned as I levered the door shut behind her.

"Good for you!" I hollered. I glanced at the busload of noisy kids through the big spy mirror above the steering wheel and smiled as big sis swiped at jelly on her brother's chin. He grimaced.

Picking up children for Sunday school enriched my soul like nothing else.

Each Saturday, I made my rounds in the Hood River neighborhoods, reminding parents and kids that our 30-foot yellow church bus would be honking at their driveway, ready to take them to church the next morning.

After promising to serve Jesus, I never hankered for my old life again — it's a miracle that I never take for granted to this day. My daughters, Claudia and I dove into the River of Life Assemblies of God church, and we worked together, helping the congregation learn and grow stronger, right along with us.

Tasting Triumph

Every nail I hammered at the church and every meal Claudia cooked, every child I hugged and every young woman Claudia befriended added to our family's heavenly trust fund. Like sweet apples on an infinite conveyer belt, blessings filled our lives.

I put my carpentry skills to work in Hood River, gradually becoming a journeyman and foreman. Claudia took employment in the office at Diamond Fruit Growers, and the four of us blossomed despite the usual threats of frost that test every family: financial ups and downs, teenage traumas, health issues.

Claudia and I set up an account at our bank, setting aside funds to supply the needs of others — like building a wheelchair ramp for an elderly widow or repairing a stubborn roof leak for a young couple.

In time, with other tradesmen, I represented our River of Life fellowship helping build two churches in Western Samoa. We helped construct the East Africa School of Theology at Nairobi and South Pacific Bible College in Suva, Fiji. By the time I was 56 years old, I had served on the church board as treasurer and taught Bible classes, too.

My girls graduated from Northwest Bible College, and I had almost 20 construction years under my belt, building homes and multimillion-dollar commercial buildings. It seemed that Claudia and I had turned a corner in our relationship and our lives. We looked forward to a quiet Hood River life, serving God at our church and living out our heritage among life-long friends.

Voices from the Valley

❧❧❧

When a carpenter fights back tears to eat his pie with a cup of coffee, it's time to see a doctor.

My dentist had wisely advised me to have someone look at a recurring brown sore on the right side of my tongue, but I had cancelled a couple appointments due to work. And Claudia and I had set a date for a long-awaited Hawaiian vacation, and I wasn't about to postpone it for a silly doctor's visit. Claudia and I flew to the Islands for a three-week luau and beach lolling, and our trip did us a world of good.

But upon returning home, on a Sunday night after church, I barely touched my generous slice of apple pie. My mouth felt like it was on fire, and I figured I better follow through with a doctor's appointment.

After my visits to a clinic, a physician held my x-ray like a stalk of poison ivy one afternoon, looking worried.

"Mr. Perkins, you need a biopsy right away."

Suddenly I got worried, too — I hadn't mentioned my doctors' visits to Claudia at all.

"I should kick your hind end, Bill! Why didn't you tell me?"

I was nailing down lame excuses in my mind as fast as I could.

"Now didn't we have a fantastic three weeks together? And you didn't know a thing about my tongue. If it's cancer, it's cancer — and even if I have three months to live, just think about the wonderful vacation we had!"

Tasting Triumph

❧❧❧

So many loose ends in my life.

Grandchildren, unpaid bills, insurance plans, building projects, church work ... my list seemed to grow every night as I lay awake thinking. My biopsy had come back positive. The sore patch on my tongue was called Squamous Cell Carcinoma.

If this sudden invasion of evil had overtaken me when I sailed to Korea aboard the *General Freeman* or when I marched with my unit in the DMZ or when I was a middle-aged father driving a beer truck, I would have fallen off a cliff of depression. I would have put on a brave front, but I would have known I was unprepared to meet God if I lost the final battle.

But I wasn't that man anymore. The author of my eternal destiny was my best friend.

The Wednesday night following the biopsy, I did what my Bible instructed: I asked the elders in my church to pray for me. I stood with several friends gathered around me, their gentle but strong hands upon my shoulders and head. Pastor touched a dab of oil on my forehead as a symbol of God's healing Spirit, and the whole congregation lifted up its voices to God on my behalf.

I stood before the altar as I had years before and felt the same sense of freedom, but this time a new layer of comfort wrapped my soul. A blanket of peace descended with an unshakeable *knowing* that God had his healing hands on me, too.

Voices from the Valley

Following the church service, a woman I didn't know very well related a vision she experienced while everyone was praying for me.

She wrote it down for me to keep:

On Wednesday March 17, 1992, during the evening service, the elders were called upon to pray for the healing of Bill Perkins. As I stood and prayed for this man I hardly know, I felt a compulsion to cleanse myself before the Lord, to make myself pure and clear the way. I began to confess my sins to the Lord, and as I did a picture came to my mind.

I saw Jesus standing in the dark, his back toward me. As I confessed my sins, I saw a light appear at his feet. The light grew and cut through the darkness to make a pathway. At the end of the pathway was Bill.

All around me stood people wailing and crying before the Lord. I stood silent and calm.

Jesus began to walk along the path to Bill. As they met, Jesus gently held Bill's tongue in his hands and began to stroke it. I saw a blackness coming from the back of the tongue. Jesus drew the blackness forward with each stroke until it came to the tip of the tongue.

During this I was aware that there was a change in atmosphere around me. The prayers had changed to peaceful, calm prayers.

Tasting Triumph

Jesus continued to stroke Bill's tongue until all the blackness had been drawn out. He took Bill's head in his hands and kissed his forehead. Jesus then turned and walked slowly back along the pathway. When he reached the place where he had started, he turned again to face Bill.

At that exact moment the elders dispersed as though they knew that it was all over. People around me calmed themselves. I heard people weeping. All I could do was smile. I felt an overwhelming peace and warmth. I felt a love for this man who I saw Jesus heal.

Isaiah 58:8: "Then your light will break forth like the dawn, and your healing will quickly appear; then your righteousness will go before you, and the Glory of the Lord will be your rear guard."

As written by Julia

I stopped by the construction office the next morning and told my boss that I thought I might have to take some time off because of upcoming cancer treatments. A shadow drifted over his face, but I smiled, reassuring him.

"You know that I believe that Jesus heals today, Don. In fact, this tumor is already shrinking."

I had noticed that the lump on my tongue had grown smaller that morning when I examined it in the mirror. The process of healing had already begun.

I went to work that day, and later Don showed up,

looking thoughtful. "Bill," he said and sat down on a set of unfinished steps. "I want you to focus on getting well. And as long as I'm in business, you have a job."

❧❧❧

Cancer treatments are all-consuming for the patient and those who are close to them. They enter a theater of war, with each mission carefully strategized before a battle. At Oregon Health and Science University, my physician first removed lymph nodes in my neck, the most likely place that cancer might spread after the tumor was removed from my tongue.

This first operation was a success, and my doctor told me, "I may have to break your jaw and spread it wide to get to the tumor. I don't want to, but it may be necessary."

When I awoke in ICU after my second surgery, the first thing I did was reach up to see if my jaws were connected. They were. The surgeon was able to go through my mouth after all, thank God. In a six-hour operation, my doctor sliced out the malignant chunk of my tongue, leaving me 75 percent of the organ.

My tongue immediately began to swell to double the size, and they installed tubes through my nose to feed me — which was terribly irritating for a man who enjoys eating as much as I do.

In all of these distasteful procedures, I can truthfully attest that I had no pain! I required no pain medication and refused it until threatened by a burly nurse.

Tasting Triumph

"Mr. Perkins," she said, "if you don't take your meds, I'll slip it into your puree!"

Claudia cooked and ground up all kinds of my favorite foods, but I'll never forget that horrid plastic bag with long, flexible straws reaching into my stomach.

The ordeal kept me at home for a time, but I had visitors, including my employer, Don. About two weeks after my operation, the tubes were removed, and my boss asked, "Are you ready to come back to work yet? I'll pay you for a full day, no matter how much time you put in, Bill."

I worked for about four hours a day and felt wiped out. It took six weeks to reach full steam — about the time my doctors booked me for radiation treatments.

My oncologist told me, "Bill, if it was up to me, I wouldn't put you through the radiation treatments. I see no sign of cancer at all."

But my operating physician wanted to be certain that the carcinoma was completely eradicated.

"Do whatever gives me the best chance of living the longest, Doc," I said.

I had too much to live for and didn't want to risk the cancer returning.

My boss scheduled all our building projects around my appointments, while I scheduled 35 radiation treatments.

Voices from the Valley

After two years of being cancer free, I celebrated with my doctors who said I had arrived at a milestone.

"Eighty-five percent of all cancer treated in the head and neck return in less than two years, Bill. You made it!"

It's been 20 years since my operations, and every time I see my dentist, he shakes his head about my "peculiar" recovery. In my first couple treatments, the radiation reflected off the gold crowns in my teeth, and I received many times more doses than normally required. It's a miracle that I have healthy gums and any teeth left at all! My dentist tells me that my gums look like I never suffered a single dose of radiation.

༄༄༄

Every few years, Claudia drags me in for a checkup, and after the examinations, we leave the doctor's office praising God for my sustained healing.

In my late 50s, I couldn't really make sense of the battle I fought, but today I see my illness with clarity. My healing was not just for me.

My whole ordeal — from biopsy to radiation therapy — invited my doctors, nurses, family and friends to experience an intimate encounter with God *with me*. I believed Jesus would provide healing care, and he showed his faithfulness.

I fought a pitched battle with a murderous foe who humbles his victims, but Jesus deployed a combination of resources — supernatural and medical — to heal me.

Tasting Triumph

This old craftsman savors the sweetness of true victory: that, while tasting the bitterness that threatened my life, Jesus touched me with unfathomable peace.

Safe
The Story of Suzanne
Written by Arlene Showalter

"Sorry, miss. Can't take you." The Air Force recruiter gazed up at me.

I stared, stupefied. "Why not?" I gasped.

"Failed the physical."

What?

"Failed?" I squeaked.

"You're pregnant. Against Air Force Regulations."

My world reeled while my heart stopped. I about-faced for the door and fled down the street. *Pregnant, pregnant, pregnant* pounded with every footstep.

An intersection approached. *Do I turn left? Right? Keep going?* A coherent decision eluded my foggy brain. But one thing I knew with rock-solid clarity.

He will *not* get this baby.

Confusion

I remember a few happy times when I was a young child. I would tiptoe to the front door of our duplex (where I lived with my mom and brother) and let myself out. The early morning sun barely peeped through the pines as I crossed the porch to the other side and knocked.

"Hello." The lady who opened the door smiled down at me. "What can I do for you?"

Voices from the Valley

"Mommy's still sleeping, Gramma," I explained. "And Buddy, too. Can I come in?"

"Of course." She swung the door wide. "Let's have a tea party."

"Gramma, you're the bestest."

"And so are you!"

She touched her finger to my nose as I passed into the house. Gramma's tea set fit my 4-year-old fingers like a dream.

All that happiness began to change when my mother brought a stranger into our fatherless home a few months later. "This is Cameron." Her green eyes danced. "We're going to go live with him."

I stared.

"Don't worry, Suzie," Mom said. "It'll be fun. A new adventure."

We moved into Cam's home in Idaho, where he was a pastor, and I started first grade.

It was only several months later when my mother informed me, "We're going back to Oregon." Apparently, Cam's church had issues with a divorced mother of two marrying a divorced preacher and father of five and removed him from the pastorate.

We returned to Oregon where I finished first grade.

Unfortunately, this time, we didn't share a duplex with Gramma.

Just one year after introducing us to Cam, Mom had divorced my father, married Cam and given birth to their first daughter together.

Safe

We weren't in Oregon for very long before she called a family meeting.

"We're moving to Montana." She kept her smile and tone bright.

"Why?" I asked.

"You're too young to understand, Suzie." She sighed. "We just need a fresh start, far from here."

My new father worked odd jobs in the city. I attended four schools in second grade as we moved from place to place and Cam from job to job.

I missed my happy times with Gramma.

Cam took seriously the admonition "Withhold not correction from the child: for if thou beatest him with the rod, he shall not die" (Proverbs 23:13 KJV). He beat me for poor grades. He whipped me for wetting the bed.

Why is he beating me? My 6-year-old brain struggled to find answers. *Why doesn't Mommy stop him?* She had yielded to his totalitarian leadership in the home.

Another sister soon joined our family.

☙☙☙

"I miss Gramma," I told Mom when I was 10. "Can't we go visit?"

"It's too expensive for us all to go," Mom said, "but how would you like to fly down?"

"Really?" My insides flip-flopped. "Just me?"

"Yes." Mom smiled. "It'll be another new adventure. Your first airplane ride."

Voices from the Valley

My eyes and heart widened. *Wow! My first airplane ride, but more important, Gramma and Grandpa at the other end.*

They met me at the airport. Four years of longing melted away in their embraces.

What a summer Grandpa and Gramma gave me. Grandpa threw provisions into his homemade camper, and we drove to camp on the coast. We visited a wildlife safari, oohing and aahing over the lions and cheetahs, bears and gorillas.

Gramma and I worked in her garden, weeding and harvesting. We munched on fresh green beans, lettuce and tomatoes. Gramma made me wonderful clothes for the next school year.

Too soon, I flew back to Montana. However, my heart was soaring as high as the airplane, full of happy memories.

Cheated

Sixteen months later, a local talk show invited my sixth grade class choir to sing Christmas carols on the air. My hands shook with excitement as I smoothed the dress Gramma made me and waited for Cam to drive me to school.

Instead, he sat down and pulled me in front of him.

"Suzie," he said, peering deep into my eyes, "you're going to be Daddy's *big girl*, now." With that he ran his large hands over my shoulders and drew me close — too

Safe

close. He lowered his head and crushed his lips against mine.

What are you doing, Daddy? Shock shot through my body and pierced my confused mind. *You should be kissing Mom this way, not me.*

I stood like a dead stone. He raised his head and smiled — a sickening, threatening, leering smirk. "It's our little secret." His face switched to warning mode. "Tell your mother and you'll regret it — I promise you."

Memories of senseless beatings warmed my bottom. I stared at his feet and nodded.

Mom left for work early every morning. After becoming Daddy's "big girl," I often woke up in *her* bed, next to *her* husband, to fondling meant only for *her*.

☙☙☙

Sometimes my stepdad's other children joined us in Montana. The house overflowed with kids, and being the eldest, Mom expected me to fill her shoes and apron while she worked, cooking, cleaning and laundering.

We initially attended an Assemblies of God church when we first moved to Montana, but that dropped off like leaves in autumn. At times, Cam held "church" for the brood roosting under his roof.

Put on your happy face, I lectured myself, staring in the bathroom mirror. *Everything will be fine. Keep the peace.*

I heard Mom welcoming neighbors who sometimes

joined us for our keep-it-in-the-home church. *Can't let them guess the truth about what goes on here.*

I released a long pent-up breath. *It must be my fault, anyway, because God's not doing anything to stop it.*

Two years passed. We drove to Oregon for Aunt Alexis' wedding. Soon after we started back for home, our van broke down, so we turned around and returned to Gramma's.

Cam flew on to Montana to get back to work. My siblings and I enrolled in the local school. A few months later, Cam had saved enough money to fly the rest of us back to Montana.

"I don't want to go," I told Mom.

"Because you've already started school here?" she asked.

I nodded. *Better than the truth,* I thought. *That would kill her.* Mom agreed, and I stayed behind.

However, at 12 years old, I missed my own family and soon flew back home. *God, can you give us a normal family life?* I gazed at the puffy white clouds billowing below the aircraft and crossed my fingers. *Maybe, just maybe, things will be different this time.*

They weren't. I awakened in my mother's bed once again to fight off probing hands and lips. Cam finally let me go when I let out a strangled scream. He stuffed bribe money into my trembling hands.

"I'm sorry, Suzie," he said. "It won't happen again."

His promises held the sincerity of a politician six points behind in the polls.

Safe

The assaults intensified. Only my screams staved off penetration.

"I'm so sorry, Suzie," Cam said. "I promise it will never happen again."

Eventually the family moved back to Oregon. Once again, Gramma's house provided some refuge from Cam's attentions.

Comfort

"How would you like to go to a Christian boarding school?" Mom asked me before eighth grade ended.

Boarding school? Away from Cam's hands and the chaos of this house.

I curbed the enthusiasm bubbling from my heart to my lips. "I guess that would be okay."

Mom's eyes grew distant as she talked of the place. "I always wanted to go there," she said. "We couldn't afford it, though."

We drove for several hours to the school in a small town to check it out. Mom enrolled me, and then the director took us on tour. We wandered over the grounds, admiring the redwood trees, the mountains standing guard in the distance, and crossed a creek that sliced the campus in two.

I'm going to live here? I wanted to pinch myself.

"Here is Higgins House," the director said, leading us to a stately three-story white building. A fountain in front completed the idyllic picture. "This is our girls' dorm."

Voices from the Valley

We moved from floor to floor of the immaculate quarters as I pondered the possibilities for newfound life.

"As you know," she continued, "this is a small community, but everything the students will need is within a few blocks' walk."

All I need is peace, I thought, *and being 100 miles from home should do it.*

For the first time in years, I felt a waft of hope.

After my freshman year began, I reveled in the tranquility that surrounded me. I strolled about the campus, inhaled the purity of the crisp late-fall air and gazed off to the mountains. *I lift up my eyes to the hills — where does my help come from?* (Psalm 121:1). I smiled. *Maybe God does care about me, after all.*

I missed my family, but not Cam's hands. And, for the first time in my life, I saw the real Christ modeled, through the teachers' kind and fair treatment, not the hypocrisy at home.

Strict rules kept us on a high moral footing. Others groaned, but I rejoiced. *Male selfishness is the last thing I need to deal with.*

I felt safe enough to make a few friends, feeling my shameful past was indeed the past and sordid secrets wouldn't be spilled at inopportune times.

I let down my guard a little. I lived. I breathed.

I even laughed!

❧❧❧

Safe

As I wrapped up my first year at boarding school, my family followed Cam and his latest job, working on oil rigs in Texas. I went there for the summer.

He busied his hands again.

I can't stay here, I thought. *I've got to get out, but where?*

"Mom." I approached her after another difficult day of dodge-the-hands. "I want to meet my real dad."

Mom shrugged. "Okay," she said. She made the necessary arrangements.

Buddy and I flew to South Carolina to meet a man I couldn't remember. *Can't possibly be any worse than Cam. I want to get to know the person I came from.*

We got off the plane. I stared at the tall, lanky, dark-haired stranger, smiling and holding his arms out wide. Buddy and I closed the distance at a run, throwing ourselves in his arms. He wrapped us together in our first family hug.

I sighed against his chest. *Now I'm complete.*

"I can't tell you how happy I am to see you," Dad said, eyes glistening behind his glasses. "I've missed you more than you'll ever know."

"Why didn't you visit?" Buddy asked.

"I would have, son," he said. "Believe me, I would have, but your mother wanted no contact, and I had to respect her decision. I couldn't put you between two squabbling parents."

I squeezed him as hard as my 14-year-old arms would allow. "But we're together now!"

Voices from the Valley

"How's your mother?" Dad asked later over Cokes and fast food.

"Okay, I guess," I said.

"I married again," he said, then sighed. "Didn't work out. I couldn't get your mom out of my thoughts and heart."

Chaos

We spent a month getting to know our father. Before the visit ended, Mom called.

"Guess what?"

"What, Mom?"

"We're living in South Carolina now."

My mind reeled.

"Who?"

"The kids and I."

"And … and …" I glanced at David, my *real* dad. *I'll never call Cam Daddy again.*

"Cam? Oh, he took a job again in Montana."

Dad drove Buddy and me to Mom's new stopping-off place, living with some friends.

"What are you going to do about school?" Mom asked.

"I want to go back to the Christian boarding school," I replied.

"Cam's making plenty of money now," Mom said, "but that's such a long way from South Carolina. Are you sure?"

"Yes," I said.

Safe

Please, God, let me return to the only stability I've ever known.

I spent the entire sophomore year there, without seeing my family.

The last day of school came.

"Hey, Suzie," a classmate yelled. "Your mom's here to pick you up."

"Mom — here?" My thoughts raced. *She drove from South Carolina?*

I ran downstairs.

Mom stood, smiling. "Surprise!" she said. "Cam and I have moved back to Oregon, and we're camping near a river. It's great. You'll love it." My heart dropped.

I didn't love the perpetual camp scene, so I moved in with my grandparents again. Fall rolled around, but this time there wasn't enough money for me to return to boarding school. I moved back with the family and started my junior year at the local public high school.

Cam returned to fondling and groping.

I found an afterschool job as a dishwasher to keep me away from the house as much as possible.

"Come on, Suzie," Cam said. "We need to shop for dinner."

I slid into the passenger side. My legs trembled as I closed the car door.

Sure enough, Cam turned onto a secluded side street, cut the engine and reached for me.

"Stop," I pled, "you know this isn't right." The door handle jammed into my back as I fought and begged.

"It's all your fault," he growled. "You know you do things to drive me crazy. You always have."

Huh?

"Go ahead," he taunted. "Tell your mom. Destroy her world."

Companionship

"Suzie," Mom called to me after hanging up the phone. "That was the Christian boarding school. They told me they offer a scholarship. You can finish high school there."

Is it possible? Is there a God in heaven who really cares?

I thankfully returned to my beloved school to start the second quarter of my junior year. I continued to have a few friends, but I never let anyone get close; I didn't really trust anyone. That all changed at the beginning of my senior year there. When I met my new roommate-to-be, it seemed that God had planned it.

"Hi." The cute girl with long, blond hair smiled. "My name's Susie."

"So's mine!"

"It's short for Susanna," she explained.

I giggled. "Mine, too."

"How fun," she said. She touched a necklace at her throat. "My parents gave me this for my birthday last May."

I leaned in to examine it.

"My birthday's May, too," I said.

Safe

"No kidding? When?"

"The second," I said.

"So's mine! Amazing!" Her smile broadened. "We're definitely meant to be friends." She hooked her arm in mine and steered me toward our classroom. That was to be the special beginning of a life-long friendship.

Susie and I also struck up a friendship with two boys, Seth and Ethan, also best friends. We four became inseparable. We attended school, sports and church activities together. I trusted Susie, Seth and Ethan. They trusted me.

I valued their friendship. I needed their friendship. They became as bedrock to me.

It wasn't long before our simple friendships blossomed into dating. Susie and Seth established a serious commitment to each other. Ethan and I grew closer, as well. We came to an unspoken understanding. *We belong together. Life is good.*

We all graduated and returned to our families, seeking jobs and further education. Susie and Seth's relationship moved quickly, and they married that summer, moving on with their new lives together. Ethan and I continued our relationship, though at long distance.

Before too long, Ethan decided he was going into the military. *What do I do now?* I cast around for ideas.

Cam cast around for me.

I took a summer office job and often retreated to friends' homes or my grandparents to keep away. Later that fall, I found a waitressing job.

I enrolled at a local community college. Ethan had already left for the military where he worked his way up in rank and responsibility.

Cam intensified his attentions.

To escape, I moved in with my grandparents — again. Nobody ever asked *why*.

At the end of that year, I flew back east to visit Ethan. My dad lived in a nearby state, so he came to visit me. We'd kept in touch through letters.

Unfortunately, I had to move back in with my family when I returned.

Cam once again returned to foul play.

"I'm done, Cam," I stated, pushing him away. "I'm sick of trying to fight you off. I'm leaving forever."

"Please," he begged. "Don't go. I promise I'll get help."

He found an excuse to leave home for a month and get counseling.

I stayed while he was gone.

What should I do until Ethan gets out of the military? I frowned at my unknown future. *School? Work?*

I decided on work and began another job search.

Confrontation

The whole family went to our grandparents' home a few months later to celebrate Gramma's birthday, which fell on a Monday. We returned home later that night.

The next day I slept in, not feeling well. I slept late enough for all the kids to leave for school and Mom for

Safe

work. I slept late enough for Cam to slip into my bed.

I awakened to the sickening, familiar, undesired feel of being groped as he pressed himself hard against me.

"Get out," I screamed. "I'm leaving right now and never coming back. Never!"

This time, he ignored demands. Instead, he pushed me down, held me down and pierced me — down to the depths of my soul, my being, my existence — and then he departed.

I lay paralyzed, alone.

Eons later, I dragged my soiled self to the shower, dressed, packed a few clothes and left. I rode the bus into town and found a clinic.

"Can I get a D & C?" I asked, trying to control the tremble in my voice.

The dispassionate clerk named a price.

I left. I had no money.

I had no hope.

I walked to a friend's house.

"Can I crash here for a few days?" I begged.

I have to get away forever, but how? Where?

I wandered around town again and stopped in front of an Air Force recruiting office. On impulse, I entered.

"I'd like to sign up," I said to the sergeant seated at the desk.

"Good, good," he said. "Age?"

"Twenty."

"Good. High school diploma?"

"Yes, sir."

"Good. We require you pass a physical and some other testing."

"I'm ready," I said.

I waited for the results of the physical, unconcerned over the results. Although in a catatonic emotional state, I had a strong and healthy body.

Eventually, the sergeant rustled the papers the assistant had handed him.

I stood up.

He scanned them and then me. A slight frown puckered his forehead.

"Sorry, miss. Can't take you."

I stared, stupefied. "Why not?"

"Failed the physical."

What? "Failed?" I squeaked.

"You're pregnant. Against Air Force regulations."

Pregnant ... pregnant ... pregnant ...

ൟൟൟ

Three days later, I dialed our home phone number and waited for my mother to get on the line.

"I want to meet you and Cam," I said and named a local restaurant. "Tonight, to talk about something very important."

"Okay," she said. "What's the matter?"

"I'll discuss it then," I said. "Six o'clock?"

"Yes."

I took the chair across from Mom and Cam.

Safe

"Well," I said, looking straight at him. "Have you told Mom what's happened?"

"No."

"Then, it's about time she knows *everything*."

Mom looked at me, then her husband and then back at me. She began to sob.

"Let's take this outside," she whispered.

We walked to their car. I climbed in the back and crossed my arms.

"Mom, haven't you ever wondered why I never want to be home?" I asked.

"No." She faltered. "I just thought you wanted to be away from all the kids or spend time with Gramma."

"No, Mom. I've been fighting off Cam since I was 11. *Eleven*, Mom." I dared to snort. "I succeeded for nine years, but … I failed," I choked. "On Gramma's birthday. And now … now I'm carrying his child."

Mom's sobs increased. Cam offered to take the child. I was horrified!

I opened the car door and stepped out. "I won't be back. Ever."

A week later, Mom called.

"I'm so sorry, Suzie," she started. "So sorry I never noticed. Believe me, I'll back you up whatever you decide to do."

Then Mom left Cam, took the kids and moved to New Mexico.

I was alone. Again.

God, where are you? Why is this happening to me?

Voices from the Valley

This must be my fault somehow. What will Ethan think of me? I'm going to lose him, too.

I felt lost, unsure, without hope and without options. I ran from my family and from God. In despair, I sought an abortion.

Compassion

Dear Ethan, I wrote through tear-filled eyes. *I have to tell you something awful, and if you don't want me anymore, I understand.* I wrote about the rape and abortion.

Dear Suzie, he wrote back. *Know that I support and love you. We'll talk about this more when I get leave. Come stay with my folks for Christmas.*

"Want to talk about it?" Ethan's voice was soft, soothing, when we finally found alone time during the holiday.

I nodded.

"Who ... who assaulted you?" he asked, putting one arm around me and holding me close.

"Cam." The years of filth and helplessness and frustration boiled together. Words tumbled over my lips and mingled with my tears. I tried to loosen Ethan's embrace.

"It wasn't your fault." He held me closer. "I still love you and want to be with you, Suzie. I feel the same as I did before about you."

Is this possible? My heart leapt. *A man who loves me*

Safe

in spite of my being soiled? A man who will not use or abuse me?

I collapsed into his embrace.

Ethan returned to base and I to a friend's home. No way would I ever go home again.

That spring, Aunt Alexis invited me to stay with her.

I think I can handle family at this distance, I reasoned. *Aunt Alexis is fun. We'll have a good time together.*

"Together things" included church.

One Sunday, Cam and several of his kids showed up. He approached me after the service.

"Hi, Suzie," he said with his usual smirk. "I'm going down to pick up your mom and kids. They're moving back with me."

I was so confused and angry, I lost it and let it show.

I can't let that happen!

"Okay, Suzie," my aunt said, coming into my bedroom that night. She crossed her arms and barred the door. "What's going on?"

I spilled the whole sordid story.

"You need to go to the authorities," she stated.

"Okay," I said, shrinking into myself.

Getting it out in the open freed me up somewhat. No more lies. No more sneaking around. No more dodging. No more hiding filthy secrets.

I joined Ethan when he came home for a 30-day leave.

"I think you should move here," he said. "With my parents. They're open to it."

I seized their offer, moved in and began attending

church with them. That fall, they took me to a church camp.

One night, a message was given about the importance of forgiveness.

Forgiveness? Is he joking? Why should I forgive Cam? I crossed my arms.

Where were you, God, when it was all going down? And what did he get for it? Six whole months in jail. Six months for nine years of abuse and rape!

I wanted to scream my anger and frustration. Even though Mom eventually divorced Cam, he remained an unwelcome fixture in my heart.

Why me, why me, why me drummed a relentless beat in my heavy heart.

"We have to forgive to be forgiven," the speaker continued.

For too long I have lived with my guilt, despair and anger. For too long I have held God at a distance. I needed to know that he accepted me, in spite of my past.

My broken heart responded.

Oh, God, I cried from the deepest part of me. *I can't forgive on my own, but I give you permission to help me forgive. I can't live this way any longer. I need you. I need your forgiveness. I need your peace. I need your love.*

A peace I'd never experienced flooded through me as God's forgiveness washed away my tattered emotional wreckage. I breathed deep, inhaling the fragrance of pine and God's love.

Safe

Cherished

Ethan's family gathered at his grandparents' to celebrate Christmas, where he took me for a walk along the creek that ran through their property.

He put a tender hand on my elbow and turned me to him. "Suzie," he said, "I'm going to ask you a question." He paused. "I'll probably ask it again later on, but, will you marry me?"

My eyes widened. *Marry you? The man who treats me right? Who doesn't view me as soiled goods? Who cherishes me?*

I threw myself into his arms. "Yes — yes!" I cried.

Ethan produced a promise ring (a symbol of pre-engagement) and slipped it on my finger. "I'm leaving for an overseas assignment soon and wanted that puppy to have a home before I go." He grinned.

"Unfortunately, it's an unaccompanied tour, meaning you can't come along," he explained. "A year and a half is a long time apart, you know. I didn't want to marry you and then leave you for so long; it wouldn't be right." He promised we would marry after he was back.

In the meantime, I continued to live with his parents, enjoying the welcome and safe atmosphere.

After Ethan's military discharge, we celebrated his return in a cozy restaurant.

"Remember when I said I would ask you a question twice?" he said, pulling something from his pocket. "This time it's official. Will you marry me?"

Voices from the Valley

I stared at the diamond resting in the velvet box.

"Yes — yes," I joyfully repeated.

Grand plans were set in motion, and we married the following spring.

Ethan pursued his career. Unfortunately, this meant working more and more hours away as he climbed the ladder of success.

Crisis

"Hi, Suzie." The man's voice on the other end of the phone sounded warm and comforting.

"Hi, Casmir. How are your girls doing?"

"Good." His voice deepened to confidence.

"How about lunch?"

What harm is there, I reasoned, *in spending a little time together? I'm tired of being alone 90 percent of the time.*

Innocent lunches and chatting about his daughters somehow morphed into a full-blown affair.

Six months later, I stumbled out of my acre-sized empty bed and into the bathroom. I stared into the mirror and gasped.

It was Cam who stared back at me. Cam. The man who'd robbed me of innocence, trust, joy.

"I am Cam," I whispered into the cavernous void of my heart and home. "How could you do something so despicable?" I raged at my reflection. "Cheat on the only man who ever loved you unconditionally? How?"

Safe

I staggered to the phone.

"I can't do this anymore," I wailed when Casmir answered. "I've cheated on the one man who's cherished me from the get-go. Please, please forgive me," I sobbed. "It's over. It's over. It's over." I hung up.

"Oh, God, forgive me!" I dropped to my knees, pouring out my heart to him. As before, God poured his unconditional, forgiving, endless love into the deepest parts of *me*.

Calm

God moved fast, providing a way for Ethan and me to relocate. Life moved on. Ethan's career advanced further. I got a great job helping at a local Christian school.

The joy kept coming. My real parents reconciled and remarried. God healed Dad of cancer and began blessing Ethan and me with children.

Ten years passed. Ten wonderful, productive, peace-filled years.

We moved again, to be closer to Ethan's job, allowing him to be home more.

"We need to find a new church home," Ethan said.

"Agreed." We began visiting area churches.

Ethan's parents had friends nearby. They invited us to Hood River Assembly (which is now called River of Life Assembly).

"May as well go," Ethan said, "seeing as how we haven't committed to a church yet."

Voices from the Valley

We drove to the simple white building, located at the address given us, and shepherded our children toward the door.

People welcomed us with open hearts and arms. *I feel like a long-lost relative.* I glanced over at Ethan. Our eyes met. *We're home!*

Closure

A few years later, River of Life Assembly hosted a Ladies Retreat. *I want to go,* I thought, reading the announcement on the church bulletin board. *I want to get closer to God.*

I went with other ladies from our church family. My heart soared with the worship and rejoiced in the messages. I bowed my head at a quiet time.

Lord, thank you for forgiving my blackest sin, I prayed in my heart. *I long to know you even better.*

"You have to come clean if you want more intimacy with me," God replied. "And if you want your relationship with your husband and children to be 100 percent whole."

"Are you kidding, God?" I gasped. "It's been 10 years. *Ten!* We have three kids. It'll only hurt them all," I argued.

God waited.

I dug in my heels.

Heaven remained silent.

After the retreat, I called Ethan at work. "How about a weekend for just the two of us," I suggested. "I've already lined up a sitter."

Safe

"Sounds great." I heard the excitement in his voice. "A weekend with nobody but my lady. I can't wait!"

I can.

We ate dinner at a fine restaurant and returned to the hotel room. The door clicked behind Ethan with sickening finality.

"Ethan." My knees turned to Jell-O, and I sank to the bed. "I've something dreadful to tell you … to confess to you."

He sat next to me, sensing the gravity in my voice.

"Yes?" He tried to put his arm around me.

I stood up, shrugging his arm off. *God, how I can tell the unthinkable to my best friend, my husband?*

I crossed the room and sank into the easy chair, needing the distance.

"I … I …"

Silence hung for a long time, like a soaked quilt, between us. I struggled with where and how to start.

"I cheated on you," I finally blurted.

Shock flooded his face.

"When?" he whispered.

"Ten years ago … when … when you were gone so much …" My words trailed away.

He sat, studying his hands. After what seemed an eternity, he stood up and walked over to where I sat. He looked down at me. Deep sorrow and yet deep love filled his eyes.

"I want you to know that I love you, Suzie," he began. He drew a long, deep breath. "And I forgive you. I just need a few days alone, to pray, and we'll talk some more. I hope you can understand."

Those days crawled by with the speed of a glacier on Mt. Hood.

Ethan returned.

"I need to know who."

"Casmir."

He sighed, rubbing a hand over his eyes.

"How long," he asked, looking away with face and eyes full of mixed emotions.

"Six months." I twisted my empty hands in my lap, dreading what might come next.

After a long pause, Ethan reached over and covered them with his own. "I appreciate your honesty," he said. "I told you three days ago that I forgive you, and I meant it. Now, the past is in the past, and we need to leave it there. Let's find a way to understand what happened but, more importantly, move on to restoration and our future together."

We talked, cried and prayed together for hours. I told him how sorry I was for causing so much pain and sorrow; how I have since recommitted my life to him and God. He shared with me the sorrow in his own heart, but also shared with me how the love Jesus has for his bride, the church, helped him reach beyond that sorrow; how deep down inside the love he had for me was greater still, that the love of God is far greater. When he took his vows to love and cherish me until death do us part, that is what he meant then — that is what he means now.

Safe

I looked into his eyes. Love, only love, shone there!

He pulled me into his arms. *Lord,* I prayed, my tear-soaked face pressed against Ethan's chest. *How can I ever thank you for this man who loves me as you do?* I tightened my grip around Ethan's waist.

How can I thank you for River of Life, where I learned that Jesus is the one true friend who can help anyone with any issue, any sin, any fear? How can I thank you for providing me two safe havens from brokenness, disillusionment and defeat?

Just love me back.

I felt God's grin warm my heart. I knew that God would restore our marriage to a richness and strength we had never known before. I reached up, touched Ethan's cheek and smiled.

Five Thousand Miles
The Story of Zoila Ramirez
Written by Karen Koczwara

"Help me! Please, someone help me!" I cried, panic rising in my chest as frantic passengers scrambled to climb out of the bus. "I'm trapped!"

The water was rising fast, and within minutes, I knew it would be too late. I tried desperately to move my legs out from under the seat, but they were completely stuck. "Help, please, someone help me!" I cried out again, my voice now near a wail. But the people only pushed by, their own faces pale with terror as they screamed and cried and clawed their way to safety.

I wriggled my legs again, but my effort was futile. The icy cold water sloshed over the seats as it rushed in. Time was ticking away. Soon, the bus would be completely submerged, taking me down along with it if someone didn't come to my aid.

It had all happened too fast. The screams … the metal scraping against metal … the screeching of the tires … and then the terrible plunge. Hundreds of feet, it felt like, barreling down the hill so fast I could not catch my breath. These were the things nightmares were made of — even Hollywood could not produce such a scene.

God, please don't leave me here, I prayed as my body grew weak. *I'm too young to die! Please, don't let me take my last breath down here! I still have so much life to live!*

Voices from the Valley

∽∽∽

I was born in 1969 in the city of David, Chiriquí, a coastal town in Panama near the Costa Rican border. With a view of the picturesque Chiriquí highlands, David is best known for its farming industry, producing tropical fruits, coffee and sugar. It was just sleepy enough to maintain a laidback lifestyle and just busy enough to draw in the tourists during the warm, rainy summer months. And it was the place I called home for more than half my life.

I was raised in a large Catholic family. We attended church several times a week, adhering to all the rituals of the faith. Though I was a typical little girl who enjoyed school and the outdoors, I knew at a young age that my life might take an interesting turn.

When I was just 8 years old, I decided I wanted to become a nun. I said my rosaries each night, reciting special prayers while using a special necklace of wooden beads as my guide. As I prayed, I believed God spoke to me and told me to join the convent when I got older. I shared my desire with my mother.

"Zoila, I know you love God very much, but you are only 8 years old," my mother replied, sighing. "You don't need to worry about such things for now. Just keep saying your prayers every day, and when you are older, you can make such decisions."

I obeyed, but in my heart, the desire did not disappear. I shared my feelings with Sister Margaret, a nun with

Five Thousand Miles

whom I had developed a friendship. "I know I am very young, but I would like to become a nun like you when I am old enough," I told her.

I waited for Sister Margaret to raise her brow and disapprove, but she only nodded and smiled. "I do believe God might want you to do just that," she agreed. "Just keep praying, and he will show you the way."

I did as Sister Margaret suggested, praying each day and performing my Catholic rituals. The desire only grew stronger.

When I was 13 years old, a group of nuns invited me into their convent. I was elated — my dream had come true! While most girls my age discussed boys, music and make-up, I prepared to trade my street clothes for the modest clothing a nun wears, called a "habit."

"Are you sure this is what you want to do, Zoila?" my father asked. "You are only 13, with the rest of your life ahead of you. You are a smart girl and could go to college someday."

But I shook my head vehemently. "I have been praying, and I know this is what I am supposed to do," I replied cheerfully.

"Well, then, we will come to visit you often," he said, pulling me in for a hug. "We will miss you very much, but we are proud of you."

The senior nun at the convent objected to my coming aboard. "She is only 13," she said hesitantly. "Too young to come here."

My heart sank. I did not want to go to high school

with my peers; I wanted to serve God in the convent. "Please, this is all I have wanted," I pleaded.

The nun finally agreed to let me join, and I packed my bags and prepared to leave home. The moment I stepped into my nun habit, I felt right at home, as if this was what I'd been meant to do my whole life. I spent my days studying, learning about the Bible, praying and spending time with the other nuns. Many were much older and had much wisdom to offer. I felt honored to be in their presence.

On the weekends, we trekked up to the mountains to teach people about God, reading from the Bible and helping those in need. We took large quantities of clothes, food and medicine people had donated and passed them out to the poor. Sometimes, we visited local orphanages, spending time with the children society had sadly cast aside. I memorized their faces as I played with them and prayed for them by name when I went to bed. It felt wonderful to be doing God's work, serving the poor, and I truly believed I would spend the rest of my life in the convent, content.

As promised, my parents visited me often. My mother supported my decision and eagerly listened to my stories, but my father maintained a disapproving scowl. "I just think you need to get out there and go to college like the rest of your peers," he said. "There is so much more to life, and I fear you might have regrets if you never explore it."

I hugged him tightly. "I know this is not what you saw for my life, but it is what I am meant to do. I hope that one

Five Thousand Miles

day you can see how happy I am and know there is no place I'd rather be."

I joined the Carmelitas, a worldwide group of nuns, and grew more serious about my duties at the convent. In 1994, when I was 25, I completed a ritual in which I declared that Jesus was my spiritual husband. The nuns presented me with my official dresses, and I fought back happy tears as I slipped them on. I was a real nun, just like the ones I'd looked up to as a young girl. I would happily serve God and my community until the day I died.

One night, after saying my usual prayers in bed, I felt God speak to me in my heart. *Zoila, I love you very much, but this is not the place for you to be. I have something else for you,* he said.

I sat up, confused. "What do you mean, God? Didn't you tell me to come to the convent when I was a young girl? Why would you want me to leave?"

But again, I felt God say to me, *It is time for you to move forward and leave the convent. I have a better place for you.*

I could not understand these thoughts; they simply did not make sense. I lay back down and began to pray. "You brought me here, God. I know I am in the right place." And I drifted off to sleep.

I continued my duties at the convent, but the thoughts persisted and grew stronger. Again, I prayed, asking God to clear things up. Surely, I must be hearing him incorrectly. What better place to serve him than at a convent, surrounded by other nuns who had devoted their entire lives to doing good works? Perhaps the devil was putting these thoughts in my mind, trying to dissuade me from pleasing God.

I shared my thoughts with the Superior Mother, bracing myself for her disapproval. "Perhaps this is your father's influence, Zoila?" she said gently. "After all, he has never been fond of you being here. Do you think that could be the case?"

I nodded slowly. "Perhaps," I agreed. "I will tell him to stop visiting for now, so that I can see if this is truly God speaking to me."

I asked my father to stop coming to the convent, remaining firm as I spoke to him. "I need to sort some things out right now," I told him. "Please do not visit again until I tell you to."

I continued to pray, and I continued to hear the same message: *I want you to leave, Zoila. It is time for you to go.*

After a year of praying, I approached my Superior Mother again. "I am confident now that it is time for me to leave. I do not know what God has for the rest of my life, but I know that I must obey him," I told her.

"If you have prayed and God has told you to go, you must go," she agreed. "We respect your decision, but we also hope you will come back and help at the orphanage sometime. Those children very much look forward to your visits."

"I would love to visit again," I agreed. "Thank you for understanding what I must do."

I slipped out of my habit and left all the clothes the

Five Thousand Miles

convent had given me on my bed, then proceeded to pack my remaining things. As I walked out the doors, I glanced back wistfully at the place I had called home for so many years. I had never thought I would leave, and now I had done it. My whole life lay ahead of me like a blank canvas, and I had no idea what came next. I only knew one thing: A voice I believed to be God's had told me to leave and promised me something better.

My father was happy to have me back home. "You are such a smart girl, Zoila. You should go to the university and get a degree. You have the ability to be a very successful professional woman," he encouraged me.

I had always been good with numbers, and after praying, I decided to enroll at the local university to obtain a business degree. My father was thrilled with my decision, and I enjoyed studying accounting. But I thought often about my friends at the convent and wondered if I would ever find such fulfillment again.

I graduated with a business degree and got a good job with the Panama Forest Department. Instead of nun habits, I now wore button-up blouses, wool skirts and high heels. I was a professional working woman, just as my father had always hoped I would be.

"Look at you, Zoila," my father marveled. "You make a good salary and are rewarded for your hard work. You can now achieve your dreams and do anything you want."

I nodded and smiled. It was true. Since starting my job, I'd been able to buy a new fancy car, new clothes and anything else my heart desired. I knew not everyone was as fortunate as me. I should be grateful for my success. So why did this persistent emptiness continue to gnaw at me every day?

My job took me all over the country, often as far up as Panama City, headquarters for much of Panama's banking and commerce. A large, bustling tourist destination, the city's vast cultural offerings intrigued me, and I looked forward to visiting each time. One muggy July afternoon in 2000, I had just finished work and prepared to make the long eight-hour drive back to the city of David when I suddenly grew very tired.

I decided against renting a car and trekked up to the bus station to request a one-way ticket to David instead.

"I'm sorry, but the bus back to David is already full," the woman behind the ticket counter said apologetically.

"Oh, is there anything you can do? I am so tired and really need to get back home," I pleaded.

The lady glanced down and then back up, sighing. "Well, there is one seat left, but it's behind the driver's seat. I'm not sure how comfortable it will be. We usually use it for the driver's assistant, but we don't have one riding on this particular trip. If that works for you, it works for me."

A wave of relief washed over me. "Oh, that's fine! I don't need anything fancy. I just want to get home." I pulled my ID and money out of my purse and wrote my name down on the list. "Thank you so much!"

"The bus leaves at 2 p.m.," the lady said. "Have a nice trip."

Five Thousand Miles

My legs were so tired I could barely drag them up the steps to the bus when it arrived. I happily sat down at the front and rested my head on the comfortable seat. Outside, a cluster of dark clouds rolled over the city, and rain began to pelt the windows. It wasn't uncommon to experience a thunderstorm in the middle of July around these parts, and I figured it would make for a pretty ride back home.

The seats quickly filled, and soon the bus was completely packed. Weary passengers flipped down the personal TVs on their seats and slipped their headphones into their ears. I had ridden these buses before and was impressed with the luxurious amenities they offered. It would certainly beat driving on the slick roads while trying to stay awake.

The bus rumbled into gear and headed off. A few miles down the narrow two-lane road, I glanced out the front window and was horrified to see a car coming straight toward us in our lane.

I blinked my eyes a few times to make sure I was seeing things right — the car was definitely going the wrong way.

"Hold on, everyone!" the bus driver called out. She honked over and over, but the car kept on barreling toward us. I gripped the seat as the driver yanked the wheel toward the right to avoid a head-on collision, but it was too late. The car smashed into the front of the bus, and everyone screamed as we heard the horrid screeching sound of metal against metal. The screams escalated as the driver lost control, and the bus plummeted down a hill, heading straight for the rushing river below.

My screams caught in my throat as my body slammed against the seat in front of me. Everything was happening too fast. There was no time to think. Adrenaline raced through me as horrified passengers screamed and scrambled toward the front of the bus. It was only then that I noticed the water, gushing in from the river below, and I realized the imminence of the situation. We had to get out quickly, before the bus was completely submerged and it was too late.

I tried to wriggle out of my seat, but I was literally trapped — during the crash, my seat had been completely pushed into the driver's seat ahead. Panicked, I began to call for help, flailing my arms as the other panicked passengers pushed their way to safety. "Please, someone help me! I'm trapped!" I cried.

But in the confusion, no one heard me. I watched helplessly as they kicked at the doors and smashed the windows to escape. The muddy water rushed in, now a pool below my feet. "Please, someone help me!" I cried again, tears streaming down my face. I had never felt so alone and afraid in all my life.

"God," I prayed, "please don't leave me here! You promised that you had something for me! Surely, you didn't mean this! Please don't let me die here!"

And then someone stopped. I looked up into the face of my rescuer as he bent down and gently tried to free me. "Just hold on," he said, pushing back the seat with all his

Five Thousand Miles

strength so he could lift my crushed legs. "I got you, I got you," he assured me, lifting me into his arms.

I wanted to cry with relief, but the pain was too bad to move a muscle. "Thank you," I managed to say gratefully.

Another woman in the middle of the bus cried for help. The man grabbed her as well and carried both of us to safety. He set me down on the riverbank, where a team of paramedics had already come to the aid of several injured people. Up above, a crowd of passersby had gathered to witness the horrific scene below. All the adrenaline I'd stored up for survival now leaked out of my body, and I became weak and lightheaded.

In my dazed state, I saw a paramedic approaching me. He leaned down to assess my injuries. "Can you move your legs?" he asked.

I tried to shake my head no, but I could not move my neck. From the corner of my eye, I saw one bloodied passenger after another being carried to safety. The scene was reminiscent of a horror movie, and I knew the images would stay with me long after I recovered. *If* I recovered.

"We're going to get you to the ambulance and take you to the hospital, okay? Looks like you're pretty badly injured," the paramedic told me. "Just hang on, okay?"

The sirens blared as the ambulance rushed down the road. I fought to stay awake, but my eyelids grew heavy, and weariness overcame me. God had not let me die in that bus; he had brought help. But my life was still in danger, and my journey was far from over.

The next few hours were a blur of doctors, bright

Voices from the Valley

lights, buzzing machines and confusion. Bits and pieces of conversations flew over my head, and in my state of shock and fatigue, I tried to take them in.

"It's the weekend ... not a lot of extra help around here ... probably gonna have to transport her to another hospital ..."

"Internal bleeding ... looks pretty serious from what we can tell ... definite head injury, broken legs, broken back, broken neck ..."

"Gonna go to the local pharmacy and get her some morphine for the pain ... it's the best we can do for now ... hope it's not too late ..."

"She's from David ... that's at least two and a half hours away ... better get her there and call her family ... she can get better care there ... gonna need long-term help ..."

The morphine took effect quickly, easing the excruciating pain as the doctors lifted me into another ambulance a few hours later. *Please, God, just let me see my parents,* I prayed as the sirens wailed again. Things were happening so quickly. Everything was out of my control. I was a professional businesswoman used to taking charge, and now I was nothing more than a weak rag doll, limp in the doctors' hands as they made decisions over my head. If the accident had not happened, I would have been home by now, safe and sound in my own bed. Now I was fighting for my life.

The paramedics transported me to a private hospital in David, where they notified my parents about the accident.

Five Thousand Miles

My eyelids grew heavy again, but I fought sleep. I needed to see my parents, tell them that I was going to be okay, assure them that I was not going to die.

The nurses had just moved me into a private intensive care room when my parents arrived. I had never been so happy to see them in all my life. "Oh, Zoila!" they cried, rushing to my side.

Their faces were the last thing I remembered before I drifted off and slipped into a coma.

❧❧❧

The light was brighter than the sun, but it did not bother my eyes a bit as I gazed at it in awe. A wonderful peace overcame me as I heard angelic voices singing all around me. There were beautiful flowers of every color all over. And most importantly, God was there. I could feel him, hear him, see him. I had never experienced anything so breathtaking and joyous in all my life, and I never wanted to leave.

God, thank you for bringing me here to see your presence, I prayed. *Is this the place you have for me?*

There was no more pain, only peace. Ahead, I saw thousands of people singing, praising God in harmony. Was this heaven? *God,* I prayed again. *Is this the place you have for me?*

It is not your time yet, Zoila, my heart heard him say. *This is the time for you to feel my presence so that you know I am your God.*

Voices from the Valley

And then I felt my body in that hospital bed. I was still alive … or was I?

"She is so strong," a voice said. "She is still holding on."

I felt someone touch me. My mother? I tried to open my eyes to reassure them that I was all right, but I could not move or respond. I was trapped between two realms. God had taken me to a beautiful place but told me it was not my time, which meant he had another plan. I was not going to die just yet.

A priest arrived to read my last rites, a Catholic ritual when someone appears close to death. I thought I heard weeping, my mother's sobs perhaps.

I am still here, I wanted to cry. *I am going to be okay!* But I could only lay there helpless as my worried loved ones hovered around me, praying that God would spare their little girl's life.

I lay in a coma for more than a month. The doctors performed surgeries on my back, neck and brain. I heard their muffled voices as they worked on me, but I felt no pain. Sometimes I heard other voices — my parents' — when they came to visit. They held my hand, stroked my cheeks and talked to me softly. I so badly wanted to reach up and kiss them, to tell them I was going to make it, but I still could not respond. How much longer would I remain like this?

God, I am your daughter. You promised you had something special for me, I prayed. *What is the purpose of all this? I don't want my parents to suffer any longer.*

Five Thousand Miles

Please let me open my eyes so I can tell them I have heard every word they've said.

One afternoon, I finally opened my eyes! The sun was streaming through the window, and several machines beeped around my bed. I blinked several times, taking it all in. I had no idea what day it was or how long I'd been in a coma.

"She's awake! She's awake!" The doctors and nurses came running in, all amazed to see me conscious again.

I blinked my eyes several more times, and everyone cheered. A happy chatter filled the room, overwhelming me in my groggy state. Beside my bed, the machines continued to beep in a steady rhythm, and the doctors pointed to the screen in awe.

"I'm Dr. Williams," a doctor said kindly, sitting at the foot of my bed. "I was your surgeon. You had us all pretty scared there for a while, young lady." He smiled. "You've been in a coma more than a month, and we kept waiting for you to wake up. Your parents said you were a fighter, and they were certainly right. I don't want to bombard you with questions when you're just waking up, but I'm going to stay in the room and observe you for the next 24 hours, okay?"

I mustered a weak smile and tried to nod my head. It was only then that I noticed the oxygen tubes in my mouth. I knew I'd sustained many injuries, and I had many questions. Had the surgeries been successful? Would I ever walk again? But there was one thing more prominent on my mind — I was hungry!

Voices from the Valley

I motioned toward my stomach and then my mouth, and Dr. Williams shook his head. "I know you're hungry, but it's going to be a while before you can eat regularly. You're going to have to start over again with many things, but you have already come such a long way. You will get there, Zoila."

My parents arrived, followed by my two close friends. They were all elated to see me awake. "Oh, Zoila, God heard our prayers! We have prayed every day for you and done our rosaries. You are alive, and you are awake!" my mother cried, happy tears streaming down her cheeks.

I finally opened my mouth to speak. "Do you have a mirror in your purse?" I asked her.

My two friends, who had been softly arguing in the corner, looked up and raised their brow. My mother slowly pulled a little mirror from her purse and handed it to me. I took a deep breath and held it up to my face. It had been weeks since I'd seen myself. The last time I'd glanced in a mirror, my make-up was carefully applied and there was color in my cheeks. Now, a pale, sickly girl stared back at me, eyes bulging from my skull, lips cracked and dry, my hair covered by bandages. *I am still me,* I told myself, but the image was haunting nonetheless.

"We should let our girl get some rest," Dr. Williams said. "You can all come back tomorrow to visit." He turned to my parents and added, "She is gonna make it and get well. I just know it."

After everyone left, I leaned back on the pillow and closed my eyes again. There was so much I wanted to know, but I was too tired to question the doctor right now. Instead, I thought about the wonderful place with the bright lights and the flowers and the angels singing in unison. I had seen God, had heard his voice clearly speak to me, had felt his presence. God had comforted me in that moment, assuring me that while it was not yet my time to go to heaven, he still had a special plan for my life. It had not been a dream, I was certain of that. It was very real, but would anyone believe my story if I told it?

֎֎֎

I spent the entire next year in the hospital. The doctors and nurses continued to discuss my miraculous recovery. I learned that during the surgeries, I had suffered three heart attacks and that my heart had completely stopped. I now knew that I had died on that operating table and come back to life.

I was unable to walk on my own and began rehabilitation to increase my strength. Each day, I made a little more progress and grew more encouraged. My friends and family who came to visit helped me out of bed and assisted me as I tried to stand on both feet. The doctors reminded me that I had come so far, that I was strong and that I would indeed get well.

One day, a man came in to visit. "My name is Dr. Soza," he said pleasantly. "I had to come see you. I was the one who helped you out of the bus at the scene of the accident."

Voices from the Valley

My eyes filled with tears. "It was you? You saved my life!" I cried. "No one else would help me, but you stopped and pulled me out of that seat! I thought I was going to die in that bus, but you saved me!"

Dr. Soza smiled. "It was the least I could do. I am so glad to see you've made so much progress. You're quite the talk of the hospital, you know. The miracle girl, they're calling you."

I laughed. "Well, I'm taking one day at a time," I said. "Thank you again for what you did."

Dr. Soza came in each day from then on to visit me, and we became good friends. He shared more details of the accident. Two men from the local university had been driving drunk when they veered into our lane and crashed into the bus. Many others had lost their lives and been seriously injured, but God had used my angel, Dr. Soza, to spare my life.

Most days, I woke up with determination, but some days I grew weary and discouraged. "God," I prayed, "I know that you are real and that you have a purpose for my life. I want to walk and get back on my feet so I can serve you. Please heal me completely."

After a year, I was finally released from the hospital. I was now steadily walking on my own, though my back was still terribly crooked, and my left leg was shorter than my right.

The doctors had done all they could do, and now it was time for me to enter the real world again. I knew it would be no easy transition. Because of my injuries, the

Five Thousand Miles

doctors felt it would be best for me to live off of disability for the rest of my life.

"I loved my work, and I would be so happy if I could return to it," I pleaded with the doctor.

He shook his head and sighed. "I'm sorry, Zoila, but you cannot return to your old work. It is too demanding for your new body. Your new job will be taking care of yourself."

I was disheartened. I had left the convent because I was so sure God had other plans for my life. Then I had attended the university and obtained a good job because I was confident that was what he wanted me to do. But now I would never return to the work that I loved. I repeated the words God had promised in my head: *I have a special plan for you.* Since God had allowed me to live, I knew I must choose to believe that he did indeed have a good plan for the rest of my life. I would just have to wait to see what he had in store.

I moved in with my parents and continued to pray about the next step in my life. One day, my old grade school friend Lorena came to visit from the United States, where she now lived. "You should come back with us to the United States," she said. "You are young and have so much life yet to live. It is wonderful there, and I think you would like it very much. What do you say?"

I laughed. "The United States?" I had never considered moving away from my family. But now that I was no longer working, a move sounded like an exciting adventure. I went to church that night and prayed again, this time being especially specific with God. "You promised that you have something special for me. I am not a nun anymore. I am a professional. You have blessed me with many things that other people want to have. If you open doors for me to move away, I will do as you wish and obey you. But if this is not what you want, please show me. I don't want to force anything, and I don't want to move far away from my family if this is not your plan for my life."

I went into the city and interviewed with the U.S. Embassy. The worker presented me with several documents, and I signed them all. "You won't have any financial troubles since you are on disability," he told me. "You are free to cross the border."

I was amazed things had gone so smoothly. I went back to the city of David and told my friends and family the good news. "I got my visa!" I exclaimed. "I am going to the United States!"

I knew I would miss my family very much. We had always been close. But I also felt this could be the beginning of the special plan God had for me. Nothing was certain, but I was excited to see what life on the other side of the border might offer.

I bought a roundtrip plane ticket to Southern California and moved in with Lorena and her husband. Southern California, with its miles of sandy beaches and sunny skies, reminded me a bit of Panama, but the summers were warm and dry, unlike the muggy, rainy ones back home. Expensive cars sped by on the freeway,

Five Thousand Miles

and flashy billboards and fancy stores dotted the sides of the roads lined with palm trees. I was 4,000 miles away from my family, another world away.

"There is a Christian Spanish radio station you might like to listen to," Lorena told me. "It's called Nueva Vida."

I was working on learning English, but I still enjoyed hearing my native language. "I'd love to check it out," I said excitedly.

I began listening regularly to the radio station. One of my favorite programs was called Changing Lives. Different people came onto the air and shared their stories of how God had changed their lives. I was intrigued and encouraged by their stories. They talked about God in a very personal way, as though he was their best friend. Their approach to their faith seemed very different than the way I had been raised in the Catholic church, reciting the rosary and saying prayers I had memorized. I had always felt comfortable talking to God and knew he had spoken to me several times in my heart, but I had always felt that at the end of the day, it was doing good things that would please God. Now I realized just how simple the message of the Bible was. Everyone on earth had done wrong things, called sin, and everyone needed forgiveness. God had sent his son, Jesus, to die on the cross in our place as the consequence of our wrongdoing, including mine, so that we could spend eternity in heaven with him. I did not need to wear a nun habit, live in a convent or recite prayers over and over to receive God's love. He only wanted one thing from me — my heart.

Voices from the Valley

One day, the radio announcer said, "If you are listening right now and know you need God's forgiveness, you can receive it by putting your hand over the radio and praying along with me." I stuck my hand out and hovered it over the radio, then bowed my head and closed my eyes. I whispered the prayer along with the announcer, telling God that I was sorry for the wrong things I had done and asking him to please be in control of my life going forward. Happy tears filled my eyes as I realized that God's promises in the Bible were meant for me. Knowing I would have a friend and a guide forever was greatly comforting.

"Thank you, God, for helping me understand what has happened in my life," I prayed. "I do believe that you brought me to Southern California for a reason. Now please show me what it is you have for me here. I want to serve you and do your work."

The announcer came back on the radio and said, "If any of you are looking for a local church, simply call these phone numbers, and we will help you find one in your area."

I picked up the phone, dialed and got the number of a church not far from where I was staying. I began attending every Saturday and Sunday and fell in love with the church and its people. Everyone was warm and welcoming, and the pastor preached about God's great love from the Bible. I began to see that God wanted to have an intimate relationship with me, that he wanted me to take everything to him in prayer and trust in him. And I experienced his love in a more powerful way than I ever had before.

I enjoyed reading my Bible and praying like I never had before. It was so refreshing to take all my cares to God, speaking to him as if he was my best friend. "God, I believe you have me here at this church for a purpose," I prayed excitedly. "I now see that I don't need the nun uniforms that people have invented to declare my devotion to you. I can serve you just as I am, as an ordinary everyday woman in this place. I am so happy that you have brought me to the United States."

I began working for some friends who owned a plumbing company, helping them with their bookkeeping and other tasks around their house. I wanted to earn enough money to buy a car so I had my own transportation. One day, while listening to the Spanish radio station, I heard about a special Christian celebration in the Los Angeles area more than an hour away.

"I would love to go to that, but I don't know how I am going to get up there," I told Lorena.

"Just pray, and God will provide a way if you are meant to go," she encouraged me.

I prayed, telling God how much I wanted to attend that special conference. Shortly after, the woman I worked for told me her two friends who were going could give me a ride. I was so grateful and expected something special from God at the conference.

I enjoyed chatting with them on the way up to Los Angeles, and I began praying silently in my heart that God would stir their hearts and draw them to him. During the conference, they both fell to their knees and admitted that they needed to ask Jesus to forgive the wrong they had done in their life and invite him into their life. My eyes filled with tears as I thanked God for using my life to bring them to this moment. I hoped that I could reach out to many more people in love and share the good news of Jesus' love.

༶༶༶

As a nun, I had vowed that God would be my only husband. But now, I longed for a man to serve God with and to start a family.

"God," I prayed, "if you are to give me a husband and a family of my own someday, I pray that you will give me a man who loves you more than he loves me. I have seen my parents happily married for many years, and I would like to have a marriage like that, too. I trust in you for your perfect timing in my life." I had learned to let go of my plans and give them up to God instead. His timing was always best.

When Thanksgiving arrived, my friends invited some of their Spanish friends over for dinner. One was a man named Saul. I enjoyed chatting with him and discovered we had much in common. His parents had been missionaries in Central America, and he had invited God into his life at a young age. He loved God with all his heart and desired to do great things for him. Before he left that

Five Thousand Miles

evening, he asked for my phone number, and I gave it to him.

Saul called me, and we soon began a special friendship that turned into a romantic relationship. I quickly learned something astounding — he was the voice I heard on the radio station! He was the announcer who ran the program Changing Lives, and it was because of his work that I had come to understand what it meant to have a more meaningful, more personal relationship with Jesus. I was blown away to see how God had caused our paths to cross and brought us together.

I loved being with someone with whom I could pray, share my heart and read the Bible. After four years, we married and continued to discuss our future. We both loved Southern California, but we wanted to be open to other things, too. I had purchased a roundtrip airline ticket when I moved to the United States years before, fully intending to return to Panama. I missed my family, but I also wanted to be just where God wanted me to be. I would go anywhere he asked me to go.

Saul got a phone call one day from a man named Carl Jacobson, who asked him to come manage a Spanish radio station in Hood River, Oregon. There was a large Hispanic population up there who needed to hear the good news of God's love, Carl said. We prayed and felt God was leading us to move north. I would miss many things about Southern California, including the warm, sunny summers and our wonderful church, but I was excited for our next adventure together.

Voices from the Valley

It was as if God provided all the finances for our move, making it very clear that he wanted us in Hood River. We quickly fell in love with the small rural town, complete with river views, sprawling hills and fruit orchards bursting with color. Saul began his work at the radio station, and we both began attending River of Life Assembly of God. I enjoyed the genuine friendships we made in the church and was impressed with how strongly the people focused on relationships with each other and personal relationships with God. It was a refreshing way to live.

I shared my story with many people I met, telling them how God had brought me back to life and led me to the United States. I also shared about life in the convent, and many were surprised to discover I'd once been a nun. I reminded them that God's ways were always best, that even when we grew discouraged and did not understand them, he was still doing something good behind the scenes.

"I hope we can reach many people here and show them God's love," I told Saul excitedly. "It is clear that God brought us here for a reason, and I look forward to what he is going to do through us, the church and the community."

"Me, too," Saul agreed. "It is exciting to sit back and wait on him to direct our next steps. We'll just have to see where he leads us next."

Five Thousand Miles

"God did a miracle today!" Saul exclaimed. "It was so amazing to see your aunt come out of her coma and wake up! God surely heard our prayers, just as he heard the prayers of your loved ones years ago when they thought you'd never wake up!"

"I am just thankful that God can use me," I replied humbly.

We had returned to my hometown in Panama to visit my family during the spring. We had heard that the good news about Jesus was spreading to many in the city of David, and I was elated to see so many of my family members invite God to be the center of their lives.

When I got word that my aunt was sick and had fallen into a coma, we went to visit her in the Intensive Care Unit at the hospital. I prayed over her, asking God to please heal her body and bring her back to consciousness. Others were there praying for her, too.

And then God worked a miracle, and she opened her eyes and woke up! Our cheers and shouts of thanks to God echoed throughout the ICU and caused quite a stir. As patients and hospital staff heard what happened, I was able to share with them about God's forgiveness and healing care. Several of them believed in Jesus that day!

The most special moment that day was when I was able to talk to my aunt about God, and she asked Jesus to forgive her for the wrong things she'd done so she could have a personal relationship with him, too.

I prayed this would only be the beginning, that perhaps God would even bring us back to Panama permanently someday so we could reach more people with his love.

As we climbed back onto the plane to return home to Hood River, I thanked God for all he had done during our visit. "Thank you for using my life to bring others to you," I prayed. I thought of my days of youth, when I had prayed so earnestly about going to serve God in the convent. He had brought me there, but it had only been for a season. When he told me it was time to leave and assured me he had something special for my life, I wondered if I would ever know what that was. After waking up from my coma, unable to walk, I had wondered again if he still had a good plan for my life. And when I boarded that plane to the United States, my future had remained just as uncertain. I was unsure if I would ever marry or have a family of my own.

But now I could look back and see how God had been weaving together a special plan for my life since the very beginning. He had brought me nearly 5,000 miles from my hometown to the special place he had for me, and perhaps he would bring me back there someday for good. For now, we would enjoy our wonderful church, River of Life Assembly, in Hood River, and continue to share God's love with the community through our relationships and through our radio ministry. I now knew that I needn't worry about the future and what it might bring. God had everything under control, and he would take care of my tomorrows. I need only trust in him for each day.

Down A Winding Road
The Story of Rob
Written by Karen Koczwara

Fifteen seconds.

Fifteen seconds too late, and I would have been dead.

I watched in horror as the flames engulfed the truck, taking on a life of their own as they snaked around it with thick red arms. Black smoke billowed into the air, and I could not stop watching.

I could have been in there.

I shuddered as the flames swallowed up the remains of the truck.

Moments later, I heard sirens, and my heart thudded with relief.

I should be dead right now…

☙☙☙

I was born in 1959, arriving on the tail end of the baby boomer era. *Bonanza* hit the TV screens in color, Frank Sinatra crooned over the radio and a loveable dog named Lassie became a household name. It was a wonderful, wholesome time to be a kid, and in my home, things were just as idyllic.

Hood River, Oregon, a tiny rural town an hour east of Portland, was the place I called home. Nestled at the base of Mt. Hood along the Columbia River Gorge, Hood River

Voices from the Valley

is best known for its acres of cherry and apple orchards, as well as a variety of outdoor activities both tourists and locals enjoy. The warm summers are ideal for kayaking, camping, windsurfing and biking, while the winters bring skiers from all around the country. Even as a young kid, I knew I was pretty lucky to grow up in this little piece of paradise.

My father held a good job at the Diamond Fruit Company, while my mother stayed home to raise my older brother and me. We grew up in the "uptown" section of the small town where our little neighborhood was surrounded by fruit orchards on both sides. We spent our summers camping all over Eastern Oregon, exploring the vast green mountains and rivers. When wintertime hit, my father hopped in his pickup truck and pulled me and my brother behind him on our sleds. And when the snow melted, we cruised the dirt roads on motorcycles until the sun went down.

My extended family lived up north, and we visited them often as well. My parents were as straight laced as they come, never smoking or drinking in our house. We were a close-knit family, and I had every reason to believe that when I grew older, I would write a similar story and raise a happy brood of my own.

I was a shy kid and didn't much care for school in my early years. I had trouble catching on in my classes, and my parents and teachers decided to hold me back a year. In junior high, I dabbled with wrestling, but I was happier playing outside with my brother or taking my dog down

Down A Winding Road

to the river than kicking a football around the school field or hanging out with my peers.

My mother was raised in a Catholic home but talked little about her faith background in our house. I attended a Lutheran church one Sunday morning and was intimidated by the experience. The teacher asked each Sunday school student to come forward and read a passage from the Bible, and I froze in my seat. It was bad enough having to speak up in class at school, but having to read the Bible in front of a bunch of strangers was far worse! I was glad when we did not return the following week.

As I entered high school, I remained unsure about what I wanted to do with my life after graduation. I kept up the best I could in my classes and stayed away from the party scene. One morning on the way to school, I ran a stop sign, which was strange because I had been on that road many times before, and swiped a pickup truck with the side of my little Ford Comet. As metal screeched upon metal, I gripped the steering wheel and hit the brakes as hard as I could. But the impact was too great, and I skidded into the ditch on the side of the road.

My heart pounded in my chest as I sat there in shock, replaying the last few seconds in my mind. It had all happened so fast — one moment I was driving down the old familiar road, and the next I was spinning out of control. I tried to squirm out of my seatbelt and climb out of the car.

"Are you okay? I saw the whole thing happen right in

front of my house!" A woman appeared at my window, her face pale as she met mine. "I called the police, and they're on their way. An ambulance should be here soon, too."

My head throbbed, and I feared I might pass out. "Thanks," I managed to get out. *This is the part of the nightmare where you wake up and discover it was all just a dream,* I told myself. *This is not really happening.*

But it was happening, and it wasn't anywhere near over. The police and ambulance arrived and whisked me away on a gurney. As the sirens whirred and the paramedics hovered over me, I closed my eyes and felt my body grow weak.

At the hospital, a flurry of nurses and doctors attended to me. "You've cut your head, so we've got to take care of that first," one nurse explained. "Do you have any pain elsewhere?"

I tried to speak, but everything felt like too much effort. They bandaged me up and then wheeled me in for an X-ray. My parents arrived after learning of my accident. My father, never one to handle the sight of blood too well, looked pale as he approached my bed.

"I'm so glad you're okay," he said, trying to stay strong. "Could have been so much worse."

I nodded. "I'm gonna be just fine."

The doctors released me later that day, and life went on as normal. Though still a bit bruised and shaken from the accident, I returned to school and resumed my activities.

Down A Winding Road

But two weeks later, the doctor called with some interesting news. "I was reviewing your X-rays, and I think we may have missed something pretty important. I want you to come back in," he said with concern in his voice.

I returned to the hospital, where the doctor performed a moving X-ray. After reviewing the results, he announced, "Yup. Just what I thought. You might be shocked to hear this, but you've actually broken your neck." He pointed to the X-rays. "See right here? These vertebrae have been separated. Frankly, you're quite lucky to be alive. This could have been much more serious."

I was stunned by his words. "You mean I've been walking around for two weeks with a broken neck?" I asked incredulously.

He nodded with a slight smile. "Amazingly, yes. We need to operate right away to fuse the vertebrae back together before the damage gets worse."

"Wow." His words sank in as I sat glued to my seat. In the movies, people broke their necks and died. The doctor was right; I *was* lucky to be alive.

The doctor performed the precarious surgery, inserting a piece of wire and some bone from my hip into my neck.

When I awoke, groggy and confused, I was horrified to discover I could not move my left leg. The right side of my body was numb as well.

"Is this normal?" I asked the doctor when he strode into the room to check on me.

He furrowed his brow. "It's probably just the

temporary effects of the anesthesia," he said. "Let's see how you are in a few hours."

But by the next morning, things weren't much better. The doctors continued to scratch their heads, puzzled by my condition. "The nerves must have been affected in the surgery," they explained. "Everyone reacts differently to such things. I'm sure you will return to normal within a few days."

My heart sank. I was nearly 18 years old, on the brink of graduation, with my whole life ahead of me. What if I didn't return to normal within a few days? What if I never walked normally again? I couldn't imagine not spending my weekends backpacking, biking and scuba diving in the beautiful Oregon outdoors. The wilderness was my playground; it would be devastating to sit inside on a sunny afternoon and not be able to enjoy it.

I returned home, and my parents helped make me as comfortable as possible. Each day, I awoke, hoping for some progress, but I was discouraged when there was none. I could not walk at all, and my right side still remained numb. Unable to return to school, I watched through the window as my peers cruised down the street, their lives going on while mine seemed to end.

"It's probably only temporary, as the doctors said," my father tried to encourage me. "You'll get back on your feet again and be able to do the things you enjoy."

But I wasn't so sure he was right. A "few days" turned into six months; school ended, and I still hadn't returned to normal. I was now able to walk, but my left leg still

Down A Winding Road

dragged, and with a sinking heart, I realized I'd never be able to do the things I once loved again. All because of that fateful morning on the road to school, my life had been changed forever.

Without the ability to release my energy outdoors, I turned my curiosity toward the party scene. I'd never had much interest before, as I'd been too busy to explore it. But as the days grew long and my boredom increased, I began to wonder about life on the wild side.

"There's gotta be more to life than this, don't you think?" I asked my best friend one day over burgers at the local drive-in. "You ever tried weed before?"

"No, but I know where to score some," my friend replied. "Wanna try it?"

I shrugged. "Yeah, why not?" A little pot couldn't hurt, I reasoned. After all, it was the 70s, the era of smoke-filled VW buses and peace for all. It would be nice to step out of my small world for a change.

My friend got us some weed, and I enjoyed the buzz I got as the smoke hit my lungs. I smoked the whole joint and then another. "Not bad," I muttered. "Can you get us some more?"

When we grew bored of smoking pot, we experimented with other drugs, including acid and mushrooms. I had little interest in drinking or the hard drugs, so I stuck with the "harmless" ones. I loved the way my body relaxed and reality slipped away when I was high. I didn't need to attend any fancy parties; I was happy with just a few good buddies and a couple of joints.

Voices from the Valley

After graduation, one of my friends suggested we get out of town. "I've heard Harrah's Lake Tahoe casino is hiring," he told me. "Supposed to be really beautiful there. Tons of outdoor stuff to do, and a pretty good social scene, too."

I had no immediate plans for college and no other real direction for my life. I loved Hood River, but a change of scenery and a new crowd of friends would be nice, and the money I could save up would be an extra bonus, too.

Lake Tahoe, with its crystal blue waters surrounded by staggering pine trees, was even more beautiful than my friend had described. I got a job as a houseman at Harrah's, vacuuming the hallways of the large casino hotel. I enjoyed mingling with the tourists, hanging out down at the lake on warm summer days and watching the snow fall and the skiers drive in when winter rolled around. But I missed home, and after a year, I decided to return to Hood River to be near my family.

But I grew restless again. Hood River was a small town, and there were not many jobs; many of my peers had moved away to find work. One day, my best friend mentioned moving to New Mexico for a bit. "One of my friends went to college there and says it's pretty cool," he told me. "You up for hitting the road and getting out of town for a few months?"

"Sure, why not?" The free-spirited vibe of the 70s had rubbed off on me, and I was looking forward to yet another adventure.

My best friend suggested hitchhiking our way down

Down A Winding Road

south. "You think anyone will pick us hippies up with these beards and long hair?" I asked, laughing.

"Ah, we're not that scary looking," he insisted, smiling. "Chances are, anyone willing to pick up a hitchhiker probably has long hair and a beard, too."

We stood on the side of the road and stuck out our thumbs, and soon we caught a ride going south. I watched as the green Oregon terrain faded into flat, barren land. When at last we arrived in New Mexico, the Northwest seemed a lifetime away. Santa Fe, with its old Spanish-style buildings and sparse trees, was certainly no Hood River, but the artistic culture was interesting, and I was anxious to check out the city.

Since I didn't plan to stay in town long enough to find work, I spent my days exploring the city and reading. I had picked up several books on philosophy and was fascinated by the content. Ever since my accident, I was convinced there was more to life that I was missing out on. It was nice just to exist, getting by from day to day, relaxing with friends and trying new adventures, but there had to be more to reality. I was determined to expand my mind and find out just what that missing piece was.

One day, instead of picking up my philosophy books, I plucked my old Bible out of my suitcase. I'd found it lying around the house years before, and though I'd never really read it, I carried it with me wherever I went, as though it was some sort of good luck charm. Now, curiosity overcame me as I flipped it open and began to thumb through the fine print pages.

Voices from the Valley

I stopped at the book of Matthew, the first in the New Testament section. As I slowly read, I was intrigued by the man named Jesus, whom God had sent as a little baby in a manger. That baby had grown up to be a carpenter and later went around telling people about God's love. He chose 12 unlikely men to be his disciples, who followed him on his travels, and he performed many miracles, causing some to fall at his feet, some to wonder who he was and others to hate and even attack him. Ultimately, he had willingly died a brutal death on a rugged cross so that someone like me could be forgiven for all the wrong things I'd done in my life. He knew there was nothing I could do on my own to earn my way to heaven, so he made a way by dying for me.

As I finished the chapter, I realized I'd been nearly holding my breath the whole time, waiting to see how the story would play out, just as if I'd watched a great movie on TV. I suppose I had always believed God was real, but I had never really thought much about what he had to do with my life. Now, as I read, I realized that God was not just some figment up in the sky, but my Creator, the one who had loved me so much from the beginning that he had sent his own son, Jesus, to pay the price for the wrong things I had done by dying on the cross. By giving his own life, I could now spend eternity in heaven and enjoy peace and hope with him forever! The story was not a nice little fable — it was the truth. And as interesting as those philosophy books were, I knew I had discovered the real key to my life's purpose. I needed Jesus.

Down A Winding Road

Right then and there under that New Mexico sun, I bowed my head and talked to God. "I've only just discovered you, but I know that I need you in my life. Please forgive me for the wrong things I've done, and help me to live for you," I prayed. "I now know that you are the only one who can bring purpose and direction to my life."

I wasn't sure what to expect when I opened my eyes, but I felt a newfound peace in my heart, and I knew I had just made the best decision of my life. I still had many questions, but at last, things no longer felt so complicated and uncertain. Marijuana and other mood-altering drugs were only a temporary way to escape reality, but I no longer needed to get high. I had found true fulfillment, and for the first time in a long while, I was excited about what the future held.

After three months, my friend and I decided to return home. My savings was running dry, and it was time to get a real job and get on with my life. We said goodbye to the sunsets of New Mexico and hitchhiked back to Hood River.

"I've never picked up anyone before," a guy said when he pulled his truck over to the side of the road to let my friend and me in. He smiled and added, "You guys look pretty harmless, though. Where you headed?"

"Back to Oregon," I replied.

As we rumbled along the highway, I realized the driver had just as much right to be as nervous as I was. After all, we were three strangers, riding side by side in the front of a pickup. I could be a murderer, for all he knew, and he could be one as well. I said a quick prayer, thanking God for getting us this far safely and asking him to protect us all the way home.

Once back in Hood River, I got a job at a gas station in town and spent my time outside work watching various preachers on TV and reading books about God. I hadn't told anyone about my experience and hadn't looked for a church. I'd only attended church once in my life and didn't have a clue as to where to start looking for one. *That will come later,* I decided. *For now, I'm just excited to learn more about God's love.*

Months later, I finally sat down and shared with my mother how I'd discovered Jesus was real while living in Santa Fe. "It was the craziest thing," I told her excitedly. "I carried that old Bible everywhere I went, and one day, it just occurred to me to pick it up and start reading. Once I did, I couldn't put it down. I guess God was just waiting for me to discover him. I really do feel like a changed person. I've been praying, and he's been showing me things as I do, like how to love others and not worry."

My mother's eyes filled with tears. "I never told you this, but I've been praying for you all these years," she said softly. "I guess I've always been kind of quiet about my faith, but Jesus is very much a part of my life, too. With all your wild adventures and travels around the country, I've put in a few extra prayers for you. I just knew that one day God would help you understand his love, and I'm so thrilled for this step in your life. He doesn't promise an easy road, but he does promise to never leave you."

Down A Winding Road

I was overjoyed to share this bond with my mother. I knew my father was not interested in talking about God; he had made that quite clear over the years. But I would not give up praying for him, just as my mother had not given up on me.

༄༄༄

At work, the pretty secretary caught my eye. She had long brown hair, dark eyes and a nice smile, and we got along well, laughing and chatting throughout the day. One day, I worked up the nerve to ask her out after work, and she accepted. We fell into an easy relationship, and I found myself more enamored by her every day.

My girlfriend shared my faith and talked openly about God. I began attending church with her and looked forward to Sunday mornings to hear the pastor explain how the Bible related to my everyday life. My experience as a child in that Lutheran church was so intimidating, but now that I understood who God was and how much he loved me, I realized that being a Christian was so much more than just reciting a bunch of Bible verses. It was an authentic relationship with a very real God who cared about the details of my life.

I proposed to my girlfriend, and we married a few months later in a small ceremony at the church's gymnasium. It was a beautiful day, and I was anxious to start our life together. While sitting in for jury duty one week, I met a man who happened to be a pastor of a local church. We began chatting, and he invited me to come visit his church. My new wife and I had discussed finding another church now that we were married, and I told the pastor I'd love to give it a try. We did and were happy to call it our new church home.

We welcomed a sweet little boy into our home a couple years after we married. I was elated to be a father and looked forward to the day when I could take my son exploring in the outdoors, as my own father had done with me years ago. I had never fully recovered from my accident and neck surgery, and my left leg only functioned at 80 percent. While I was disappointed to never scuba dive again, I still enjoyed taking in nature whenever I could. I hoped my son would someday see just how lucky he was to have been raised in such a beautiful town.

Another son arrived two years later. He brought added joy to our home, and for a while, life felt complete. But my wife's unhappiness soon became apparent. She grew withdrawn, and when I tried to reach out to her, she lashed out at me.

"What am I doing wrong?" I asked, desperate to make things better. We'd had such a good relationship in the beginning; where was this despondent behavior coming from?

"Just leave me alone, okay?" she retorted, storming out of the room.

We continued to attend church, and I prayed like I never had before, asking God to restore the harmony in our home. I pored over my Bible, memorizing verses that

Down A Winding Road

encouraged me when I felt down. Meanwhile, I tried to put on a brave face for the boys, taking them to their sporting activities and helping them with their homework. But the tension between my wife and me only worsened.

Our friends at church prayed for us, placing their hands on our shoulders as they asked God to heal our marriage. I was grateful for their support and thankful for my faith, as I couldn't imagine going through such strife without my hope in God.

She suggested counseling. During our sessions, she admitted her relationship with her father had affected her negatively over the years. She then also admitted she'd had an affair.

The news hit me like a locomotive traveling at full speed. I sat frozen in my chair, my heart thudding as I absorbed her words. *An affair. With another man.* "How could you do something like that?" I cried when I found my voice at last. "Don't you love me at all?"

"I'm sorry, it just happened. You and I, we were drifting apart ..." Her eyes welled with tears.

"You told me to leave you alone, give you space. So I did just that!" I returned, my voice rising as a lump formed in my throat. "What was I supposed to do? I thought we were trying here, but it looks like you gave up on us a long time ago!"

Our marriage, which had been limping along like a wounded dog for the past several years, now came to an abrupt halt. My wife announced she was done, that she no longer felt like trying. Weary from years of fighting,

Voices from the Valley

praying and begging her to give me a chance, I let her go.

My heart cracked in half as my wife packed her things and walked out the door, taking our two young boys along with her. I would see them often, but things would never be the same. Our home had been broken, and there would be no happily ever after.

"God, what am I supposed to do now?" I cried. "I'm trying to follow you and do the right thing! You know I fought for my marriage, but she gave up on us. How can I be okay with this?"

Just as I felt my thoughts start to slip into a negative place, I quickly pulled myself out of the pit. I realized I'd come to an important crossroad, and I could go one of two ways. I could spend the rest of my life feeling sorry for myself, wallowing in pity and staying angry with my wife, or I could choose to forgive her and move on. Forgiving her did not mean saying I was okay with her choice; it simply meant giving my hurts over to God and allowing him to heal my broken heart.

I returned to the book of Matthew, the one that had jumped out at me when I first picked up that dusty old Bible in Santa Fe. In chapter 18, verses 21-22, I read an exchange between Jesus and one of his disciples, Peter: "Then Peter came to Jesus and asked, 'Lord, how many times shall I forgive my brother or sister who sins against me? Up to seven times?' Jesus answered, 'I tell you, not seven times, but seventy-seven times.'"

Seventy-seven times! Could Jesus really mean that I should never give up forgiving, as hard as it might be

Down A Winding Road

sometimes? "God, that's not an easy thing to do. But since you have forgiven me for hurting others, I suppose I should also forgive my wife for the pain she caused me. Help me to stay focused on you and not lose heart," I prayed.

After work, instead of inviting myself to a pity party, I watched old movies that made me laugh. I decided that I would not let any discouraging, negative or unhealthy thing in my path. Bitterness and negativity have a way of festering deep in a person's wounds, and I wanted no part of that. I had seen many others go through divorce and turn angry at God and the world, and I wanted to be the exception to show that God restores lives and brings peace in the midst of pain.

I took a job as a propane truck driver and used the time spent on the road praying. My life had not turned out as I'd expected, but it was time to write a new chapter now. I thought back to my accident as a teen, when I'd been so sure my life was over after my surgery. Not being able to explore the outdoors as I once had seemed like a death sentence. But God had still given me a full life, and he had not abandoned me when my spirits grew low. He would not abandon me on my new journey, either.

One afternoon, while driving the propane truck on Highway 26, a car swerved out of nowhere and clipped my back tire. The truck spun out and rolled 360 degrees, and I held on with all my strength as my body flew against the seatbelt. "Jesus, help me!" I cried into the air.

Moments later, I awoke from my temporary

unconscious state. *I had better grab my paperwork.* Looking around, I heard a loud *swoosh* and watched the entire cab of the truck explode in flames. Racing with adrenaline, I lunged for the cab door and leaped from the truck. I stood there, trembling and terrified as I watched the smoke curl into the air and the fire lick the truck until it was nothing more than an unidentifiable black object.

I could have been in there. I could have been dead, I told myself, shuddering as the sirens wailed in the background. I'd seen the badly crushed cab just moments before it set fire; I could have been crushed along with it. But I hadn't been crushed, and I was still standing here, alive. Badly shaken, but alive.

The ambulance arrived and whisked me away. The doctors at the nearest hospital checked me out and treated me for a small first-degree burn before sending me home. I later learned the car was a 1987 Mustang and belonged to a guy who was high on meth. He had been on his way to visit his parole officer when he grew extremely agitated and crashed into me. I knew things could have had a very different ending for me that afternoon, and I was grateful to God for sparing my life yet again.

"I guess you're not done with me," I told God as I prayed that night. "Thank you for watching over me. I know you heard my prayers when I called out for you."

As I drifted off to sleep that night, I thought about my mother, who had prayed for me all those years without me knowing. I now knew that there was power in those prayers, that God had heard every one of them and had

Down A Winding Road

guided me in the right direction when I'd lost my way. My journey was not over; in fact, it could be just the beginning. I just needed to remember that God had it all under control.

❧❧❧

"My wife left me. Just up and told me she didn't want to be married to me anymore," my despondent friend shared with me one day after church. "I don't know what I'm gonna do."

"I know this feels like the end of the world. I've been down this road before, and it's painful," I told him empathetically. "But I can assure you that if you don't give in to bitterness, that if you give your hurts to God and focus on him, he will help you through this difficult time."

"Thanks, man, for being there for me," my friend said through his tears. "It means a lot."

I was grateful for the opportunities I'd had to share my journey with others since my divorce. I'd leaned into God when discouragement threatened to overshadow my joy. I knew how my friend felt, for I had been in his shoes one dark day years before. But I now had a new hope in my heart, as well as purpose and direction as I trusted in God's plan for my life.

I continued to pray for my father, that he would one day fall in love with God as I had. My brother was now a dental technician in Bend, Oregon, with a family of his own. And after all my wanderings as a young man, I'd

Voices from the Valley

stayed settled in Hood River, raising my boys, working as a propane truck driver and enjoying River of Life Assembly Church. Each Sunday, I looked forward to a great Bible message from the pastor, and our growing congregation had just moved into our new building. I had made many great friends along the way who encouraged me, laughed with me and shared their lives with me. My ex-wife and I were on cordial terms, and I was grateful that I had not let bitterness overtake my heart.

A crisp breeze stirred up the air as I headed home after church, as though hinting at something good to come. The fruit trees were in full bloom, and soon the tourists would arrive for the summer for kite surfing on the river. In Hood River, the seasons sometimes changed overnight, the last of the winter snow melting on the ground just as the first tree burst into color the next morning.

A little like my life, I told myself as I turned the corner toward home. Some seasons had been long, dark and uncertain, but in the morning, the sun shone again, and then, just like that, it was spring. There would be more seasons to come, but I would be ready for them. I would keep walking this winding road with God, and he would show me the way.

A Wonderful Life
The Story of Marlyn Rovig
Written by Arlene Showalter

I dove into the icy water and probed its murky depths with tense fingers. After surfacing to snatch a gulp of fresh air, I dove again. Seconds passed, crawling like a turtle on a stroll, as my search intensified.

Where ARE you?! Adrenalin pulsed through my body as I searched. My toe nicked something soft.

"Help!" I yelled. "He's here!"

❧❧❧

I was born at the local hospital, which, in 1947, occupied the second floor of the local grocery store in the pint-sized town of Plentywood, Montana, a mere 16 miles south of Canada and twice that to North Dakota.

Dirt roads, perfect for cycling, parted the rolling hills into fields of wheat and corn, and wind-bleached buttes jutted from the earth nearby. Local stores provided anything the townsfolk needed, including my favorite — a Dairy Queen.

What more could a young boy wish for?

Peace.

My parents' endless squabbles clashed with Plentywood's idyllic setting. Peace on earth. Hell at home.

I gotta get out of here. I clapped my hands over my

ears and dashed for the door. My younger brother, Orren, met me on the porch. We snatched up our bikes and raced each other down Main Street, searching for some buddies to hang out with until the heat dissipated at home.

We pedaled past the theater, my dark haven of dusty velvet seats, where, for 25 cents, I could shut myself away from familial bickering. Title and contents of the movies were secondary to escaping the battles on the home front.

As I rode, I scanned every curb, always on the lookout for a tossed bottle or can which converted to hard cash for candy and theater tickets. Canadians, who drove into town for the weekend, always left me a lucrative pile.

Next, we passed the Ben Franklin, our local five-and-dime store, always filled with interesting items, tantalizing enough to coax a few coins from a boy's pocket. Mom worked there as a clerk.

༺༻

"Here he comes," Orren whispered. We all sank down into our beds as we listened to Dad pounding up the stairs of our house, where his five children cowered in terror. His feet grabbed two or three risers at a time. Our hearts thumped.

I hope I don't pee my pants.

I had great respect for Dad's feet, recalling when one well-placed kick had sent me airborne until I crash-landed against the opposite wall. We all experienced the business end of Dad's wrath.

A Wonderful Life

Dad owned a prosperous excavation/construction business. He also had a concrete factory on the side, building septic tanks and well pits. But booze liquefied his profits, so Mom tried to keep her brood fed and clothed with her five-and-dime paycheck.

"Why do you stay with him?" I once asked.

Her sad, careworn eyes searched mine. "Because he told me if I ever left him, he'd kill me," she said and sighed.

"When did he say that?" I asked.

"Two weeks after we married."

Anger simmered in our home like jars in water baths at canning season. Dad thumped on us. Frustration drove us to thump on one other, sometimes with the aid of knives.

My first day of school began a hate affair between education and me that lasted 13 years — I repeated first grade. Classmates called me Ichabod Crane, or Icky for short, because of my skinny, lanky frame, or Shovel Feet for my long appendages.

Worse than any physical anomaly was the fact that I possessed no memory. Zilch. Nada. Zero. My grades tended to rest comfortably at the lower end of the scale.

Except one time.

Mom and I stayed up late one night while she helped me study Biology terms. After taking the test, I stared at my score. I snagged a B.

B, as in Once in a Blue Moon.

The Beatles hit the American music scene, and soon

we were all Beatle clones, blaring away on our guitars and screaming rock lyrics. I wrote many songs, and I longed for a career in music, but knew it was out of reach.

Dad was a mean drunk, but a good instructor. He taught me how to build forms for pouring concrete. I worked with him after school and full time after graduation.

"Got us another grave to dig," Dad announced at breakfast. He had the backhoe. We got the business.

I hate frozen flesh, I thought, as snow and wind whipped against the truck. Dad eased it into first gear and inched it out of the yard, turning in the direction of Plentywood Memorial Cemetery.

I manned the backhoe while Dad stayed in the truck, running the motor to keep the cab warm. When my nose turned white, I dashed over to the truck, and we switched places.

Dad finished digging the required 8x6x4-foot grave, and we switched places again. I jumped into the hole with a flat spade bar to square the corners.

"Can't get these frozen hands to move any faster," I grumbled to my audience of me-alone-in-the-hole. "But at least the wind isn't cutting through me down here." I tried to shrug deeper into my worn parka.

When my hands refused to cooperate for one more stab, I clambered out and handed the spade to my father. He finished the squaring off and waved the shovel. I lowered the backhoe bucket to help him out.

Besides working together, Dad and I sometimes

A Wonderful Life

hopped the town bars where he schooled me in the art of intoxication. When we returned home late after one of these father/son sessions, Dad discovered an unwelcome, smelly calling card, left by my terrier.

He jerked the dog into the air and held him suspended by his neck. His screams of rage mingled with Skippy's yelps of terror.

"Let go," I said.

The shrieking duo continued.

"Put Skippy down," I demanded, in a louder tone.

No response.

"Let him go, you son of a b****!" I screamed, this time topping the noise.

Dad's eyes widened, and he dropped Skippy, but he came after me bellowing like a castrated bull and swinging his fists. I threw up my arms to block the punches, but he whacked me one in my face.

Shock enveloped his face. He backed off.

"Come back, you b*****d!" I wanted a piece of him now. I ached to feel his flesh against my fist. "You son of a b****."

Dad lunged again.

Orren, awakened by the commotion, dashed into the kitchen and separated us.

Dad leaned against the kitchen sink, panting. He didn't take my bait a second time.

ಬಬಬ

Voices from the Valley

"Hold it steady," the surveyor instructed. I took a job as surveyor's helper with Hunt Oil, working with a seismograph crew. My job was to hold the pole level exactly two-tenths of a mile from the surveyor.

"Yes, sir."

A year later, the crew foreman approached me.

"We're moving on to New Mexico," he said. "Going to survey the southeast corner and on into Texas. Want to join us?"

I gotta get away, I thought. *I'm fed up with all the bickering.* Orren had already moved to Texas. I'd be closer to him.

I marinated in boredom under the hot Texas sun, but maintained a thankful heart. *No need to outrun Dad's fists here.* I dry-docked my skill of flight-or-fight until ...

"Holy Cats!" I roared, petrified. I dropped my level rod and shot across the parched land faster than a fighter jet. I'd escaped the fangs of an irate rattlesnake by a breath. *Maybe I should be a bit thankful for my childhood sprint training — running from Dad's temper.*

The conflict in Vietnam escalated. Orren and I were drafted. We drove to San Antonio for our physicals. Orren flunked due to ear problems. I flunked for a heart murmur and back problems.

"Marlyn Rovig." The doctor called me into his office. "Son," he said, "you're disqualified from service because of your health problems."

A short time later, the North Vietnamese launched the Tet Offensive. *Probably would have been in the middle of*

A Wonderful Life

that mess, I mused, watching the news. *Good thing I didn't go. Folks tell me tall people make big targets, especially if they forget to tuck their heinies in.*

"What do you think about a trip home?" Orren asked me in the summer of 1968.

"Sounds good," I replied, "but do you think our old car can make the trip?"

"I know she's a bit road-shy," Orren said, laughing, "but I think she'll pull through all right."

We started out, driving day and night. I settled in the passenger seat for a snooze.

"Hey, Morley," Orren said, using my nickname as he shook me awake. "Somehow, I got lost, but this is sure a cool area."

"Where are we?" I rubbed my eyes and yawned.

"Dodge City, Kansas."

"At a cemetery?" I asked.

"Yeah, Boot Hill," he answered. The name came from the fact that so many gunslingers lay buried there, having died "with their boots on."

We got out and wandered among the scattered wooden markers.

"Look at this," Orren said. He leaned forward to make out the words. "Says this guy took a pot shot at Wyatt Earp. He was buried August 1878." He paused and leaned closer to read more words carved into the wind-battered wood marker. "Let his faults, if he had any, be hidden in the grave."

We shared a laugh and moved on.

Voices from the Valley

"Here's an interesting one," I said and read: "A buffalo hunter named McGill who amused himself by shooting into every house he passed. He won't pass this way again. Died March 1873."

We hooted. "Guess he learned his lesson," Orren joked. "Here's another one. This dude got shot on January 17, 1873. Says, 'He drank too much and loved unwisely.'"

Orren's 1953 Chevy took its cue from the area, blew a valve and died. We resuscitated it enough to go hippity-hopping and popping back to Montana. We discovered our parents' marriage hanging by a frayed thread.

Dad put me to work, and soon I had saved enough to buy my first car. Need for speed as a young boy, sprinting from Dad's impromptu eruptions, developed into a passion for all things fast. Motorcycles replaced my old bicycle, and I purchased a 1967 Pontiac GTO with a 400-cubic-inch engine that begged to race local boys and dodge the local heat.

Dents, dings, scratches and crumpled fenders from numerous freak accidents reduced my light green beauty to ugly duckling status in a single year.

Unable to afford both repairs *and* car payments (I spent the insurance money on rent), I had to send the car back to the lender.

The nonstop parental squabbles pushed me to live with my sister in Denver. I'd stayed there a year when Mom called.

"I'm leaving your father," she said. "I can't take it any longer."

A Wonderful Life

"I'm glad, Mom," I said. "I don't know how you lasted this long."

"I want to move near my sister," she continued.

"Aunt Jean, in Nampa?" I asked.

"Yes," she said.

"I'd like to join you in Idaho," I said.

"I would like that." Mom sounded pleased. "The two youngest are coming, too."

To the family's dismay, Dad followed us to Nampa a short time later and started up another concrete business. He came over one night to fight with Mom over past peeves, and as usual, booze fortified him.

He screamed at Mom and started pushing her around. Mom ran into the bathroom, but before she could slam and lock the door, he shouldered himself in and shoved her into the bathtub.

I ran in and pulled him off before he could hit her.

Dad departed. They divorced.

ಈಲಿಲಿ

Aunt Jean came over for a visit when I was 24.

"Do you know Jesus as your Savior, Marlyn?" she asked.

"Huh?" I replied.

Mom had taken me to the Lutheran church when I was very young, but as the sibling count grew, Mom sent Orren and me, while she stayed home with the younger children. Each Sunday she gave us a quarter apiece for the offering plate. Unfortunately for God and the church, we passed a little grocery store on the way that had more tempting items, such as candy bars and soda, so the store owner often ended up with our offering.

"What does that mean?" I asked Aunt Jean.

"It means you recognize that God alone is perfect, but Jesus bridged the gap between us and God by dying on a cross so we can have a relationship with God," she explained. "Would you like a relationship with God?"

"Sure."

She guided me through a simple prayer.

"Now, your heart is clean." She smiled. "You are part of God's family now."

Aunt Jean looked happy, so I smiled, too.

I started attending a Lutheran church again. This church held a Bible study every Thursday night. The group met in the basement and sat around a large table.

Several weeks later, I spotted a new girl and sat down directly across from her. She seemed a little short compared to my 6 feet 5 inches, but she was quite attractive. I couldn't keep my eyes off her.

"I met a girl at church tonight," I told Mom when I got home.

"What is she like?" Mom asked.

"Really cute," I said, "with long, dark hair. I introduced myself, but she didn't seem very impressed."

"I don't blame her," Mom stated. "Look at you. You look like a hippie-mortician with your scruffy hair and old suit."

A Wonderful Life

"Really?" I glanced in the mirror. *Hmmm. Maybe I do look a bit shabby.*

I tidied myself up for the next Bible study, hoping Cindy would be there again. She was.

"Would you like to go walking with me?" I asked.

"Sure," she agreed.

The next Saturday, we hiked the local hills.

I worked hard to impress Cindy.

"Look at this," I said, holding up a harmless 5-foot garter snake.

"What are you going to do with *that*?"

"It makes a nice tie, don't you think?" I asked. I draped it around my neck for the duration of our trek. We drove to a nearby store for sodas, and I sauntered in, sporting my novel neckwear.

On another date, I took her to a special place I'd discovered.

"You can hear hundreds of frogs here," I explained as we found a comfortable spot to hear the concert. The entire amphibian section forgot to show up.

Once, I drove her to Silver City Ghost Town in the Owyhee Mountains. We fell in love at Mach speed hiking those sagebrush-dotted hills.

I stepped behind Cindy and wrapped my arms around her.

I've got something important to say, but I can't look into her eyes if her response isn't what I want to hear.

"Cindy." I took a deep, deep breath and rested my chin on top of her head. "I love you."

"I love you, too, Morley," she said.

I let my breath go like the whoosh of a busted tire. "Well, then," I paused, "of course you'll marry me."

"Of course."

No standard issue ring would fit Cindy's slender fingers, so we drove to Boise to order one. Our wedding day arrived without a phone call assuring us her ring was sized and ready. Desperate, we dashed the 20 miles to the jeweler's hoping to find it ready and get it to Nampa in time for our evening ceremony.

"Sweetheart, I have a confession to make," Cindy began, with a huge grin.

"What's that?" I asked, keeping one eye on the road and the other on the rearview mirror. *Don't need to complicate this day with a speeding ticket.*

"Remember the night we met?" she asked.

"Remember!" I hooted. "I couldn't keep my eyes off you."

"I know," she said. "I was peeking through my bangs the whole time."

"Unfair."

"And another confession," she said. "I want to start our marriage clean."

I glanced at her.

"Remember how I'd always call you and ask if you'd take me to church?" she continued.

"Yes." It was more a question than answer. *What's she getting at?* Concern crept into my stomach, but her widening grin calmed me.

A Wonderful Life

"My mom asked me every week, but I always told her you were taking me … then I'd call you to confirm."

I chuckled and pulled her close. "I'm glad you roped me in, babe," I said.

We collected our rings and sped back to Nampa. Folks had begun speculating that we'd eloped, until we strolled in, a mere 30 minutes late.

☙☙☙

Franklin Roosevelt's Civil Conservation Corps (CCC) constructed a lake, just outside Nampa, in the 1930s. A camp was set up for the workers and wooden barracks built to house them. After they completed Lake Lowell, the men moved on, and the barracks were sold off.

Our landlord bought one, transferred it to Nampa and remodeled it into a duplex. We built our first connubial nest in one half. Our gas heater had two settings: on and off.

"I wish I could give you better," I grumbled. "We're either roasting or freezing."

"We're together," Cindy soothed. "We're happy."

Cindy got pregnant soon after we married and stayed sick through the first two trimesters. I continued to work for my dad like before, setting forms for concrete, while he rustled up more jobs or drank. *At least the fights have stopped.* I pounded in another nail. *I appreciate that.*

Cindy's due date came … and went. We waited. Labor came, fast and hard, three weeks later. We dashed to the hospital, and the nurses took over, hooking her up to machines and prepping her for the birth.

"Can't find the heartbeat," one said. "Call the doctor, STAT!"

He dashed in. "Get her into emergency," he barked. "We'll have to do a Caesarean."

I stood, numb, watching the caravan speeding down the long hall before the double doors swallowed it, with Cindy's loud prayers trailing behind.

A nurse hustled me to another room to prep and wait.

Ominous silence flooded the room when the doctor lifted our daughter from Cindy's belly and handed her to a nurse, who cleaned and wrapped her. She handed me the precious bundle.

I pressed her still body to my heart, stroking her black hair and long, long fingers; my beautiful, perfectly formed baby girl.

Cindy awakened from the anesthesia. Our eyes met.

"She's dead, isn't she?"

"Yeah."

We returned to our empty home. Neither of us blamed God for Rose's death, but I knew Cindy hurt deeply, and I had no clue how to comfort her. *I just need to stay clear and keep my foot out of my mouth.*

We began to bicker over little things. As I sliced watermelon in our miniscule kitchen, Cindy walked in. Her eyes zeroed in on a quarter-sized drop of watermelon juice on the floor.

"You're slopping up my clean floor!" she screamed.

A Wonderful Life

"You think I have nothing better to do than clean up after you day after day?"

I looked at her, stunned, and placed the knife on the counter.

Her face crumpled.

"I'm sorry," she sobbed. "I'm so sorry."

I gathered her in my arms and drew a deep breath. "I think we're both mad at the situation," I said.

"Yes, yes." Her sobs intensified. "We need to turn it all over to God right here, right now."

We got on our knees, together, in the kitchen. My heart searched for words. At that moment I realized I had more church in my life than Jesus. *I need to get more real with God,* I thought while Cindy poured out her heart, asking God to help and heal us.

Soon, Cindy got pregnant again. She never relaxed until Shaun's lusty squall filled the birth room. *That racket is the sweetest sound I've ever heard,* I thought, recalling the silence of Rose's birth.

However, he contracted pneumonia right way, and the nurses whisked him off to the neo-natal unit and tucked him into an isolette. Cindy got to touch him first, through the protective covering of the incubator, but, again, I was the first to hold our baby.

I hugged my son to my chest — and breathed. *Thank you, Father God, for a live, healthy son.*

Shane joined our family three years later, in 1977. My father died later the same year.

Suddenly I longed to return to my roots in

Plentywood. Cindy agreed, so we packed up our toddler and baby and moved.

I quickly found a job.

"It's not what I expected," I grumbled to Cindy a few months later, when I got home from work.

"What isn't?" she asked.

"The foreman is all smiley at church," I said, "but he's a miserable terror on the job. I don't know what I expected by moving back, but I'm not getting anywhere here. Let's go back to Idaho."

"That's fine," Cindy said. "We can start planning after we visit Grandma in Oregon. Who knows?" she added, "you might find good work there."

I did.

"So, where shall we live?" I asked. "Idaho or Oregon?"

"This seems to be a great place to raise children," Cindy said.

I nodded in agreement.

She grinned. "Oregon it is, then."

I got a job driving a cement truck and then moved on to a logging job.

After three years, I took a job with a road crew, building roads through the mountains. I kept that job until an accident in 2006 forced me into disability.

"I got another job offer," I'd tell Cindy several times over the years.

"Where," she'd ask.

"They're building a road in …" and I'd name a distant location. "Big money."

A Wonderful Life

"You want it?" she'd ask.
"You know the answer," I'd reply.
"Family first," she said.
"Always," I responded.

☙☙☙

We'd been attending an Assemblies of God church in Idaho and decided to find one in Oregon, where we now lived.

After attending Parkdale Assembly for about a month, Cindy announced she would like to get baptized.

"I know we both were baptized as babies," she said, "but I want to be baptized as an adult to symbolize my decision to follow Jesus."

"Sounds like a great idea," I agreed. "Think maybe I will, too."

Cindy's mouth hung open like unbuttoned drawers.

"Remember, I told you before we left Montana that I needed to get even more serious about God," I explained. "Baptism seems to be a good way to start off by showing my decision to everyone, don't you think?"

Some of the ladies at Parkdale Assembly gathered for a Bible study, meeting in different homes each week. I began attending with Cindy because of a temporary layoff. I enjoyed interacting with the ladies and learning more about the Bible at the same time.

One week, when it was our turn to host, Cindy had to attend a preschool event with Shaun. That left me at home with our spitfire 3-year-old Shane and our newborn son, Shannon.

"You can do it, sweetheart," Cindy said. "I'm sure the ladies will be delighted to help you keep Shane under control and cuddle the baby while I'm gone."

During our meeting, Katie Miller stood up. "I feel God wants me to pray for you, Marlyn," she said, "right now."

She crossed the room, placed her hands on my head and prayed. Suddenly, out of my mouth flowed beautiful, heavenly sounds as I spoke in a language I didn't know. My heart overflowed in love and thankfulness to God.

Lord, I'm ready to learn more about you in the Bible, I prayed in my heart, *only I need your help. You know how hard it is for me to read and retain anything. I need your help to memorize.* I clutched my open Bible to my heart. *Please do something special with me. Please help me to know the scriptures, and help me understand your heart.*

A few months later, I went to the front of the church to pray after the service. John McCarty came and knelt beside me. He prayed for a little while and stopped. "Marlyn," he said, "I feel the Lord is going to use you in a big way, but you have to go through great hardship first."

I felt no fear and tucked his words away and pondered it in my heart.

ཨོཾ ཨོཾ ཨོཾ

The boys and I hurried to pack our car with camping gear. The church had sponsored a father-son campout,

A Wonderful Life

and I looked forward to spending quality time with my three sons.

"Can we stop at the store on our way?" Shannon asked. "I want to spend my bottle money."

He and I often searched for bottles and cans together, and I savored every moment spent with my 12 year old.

"Too bad we don't live in Plentywood so you can collect those mountains of bottles the Canadians always left me," I'd tease him. "We have to work a little harder here in Oregon."

Shaun drove the car, and Shane sat up front with him. We waited while Shannon went in to make his purchases. He returned with an armload of sweet loot and climbed in the backseat with me.

"Here you go," he said, passing some candy bars to his brothers.

"Thanks, Shannon," the boys chorused.

"You have such a big heart," I said, ruffling his hair.

"I wanted to get lots to hand out at camp, too," he said. His eyes grew thoughtful. "Isn't there some place in the Bible about Jesus healing a bunch of guys and only one went back to thank him?"

"That's right, son," I said, pulling out the little pocket Bible I always carried. "It's in Luke, chapter 17." I turned to it and began reading at verse 12. "As he was going into a village, 10 men who had leprosy met him. They stood at a distance and called out in a loud voice, 'Jesus, Master, have pity on us!' When he saw them, he said, 'Go, show yourselves to the priests.' And as they went, they were cleansed. One of them, when he saw he was healed, came back, praising God in a loud voice. He threw himself at Jesus' feet and thanked him."

"I always want to be thankful to God," Shannon said, "because he gives so much to me."

We arrived at the Frog Lake Campground, and the boys scattered. Unconcerned, I kicked off my shoes and, savoring the feel of cool dirt under my feet, joined some of the men sitting at a picnic table.

Thank you, Jesus, for my boys. I breathed deep the fragrance of the pines. *You've filled my life with my responsible Shaun, rambunctious Shane and gentle, quiet Shannon.*

"Mr. Rovig! Mr. Rovig!" a young boy screamed as he dashed up to me. "Come quick!"

I jumped up, my stomach already churning.

"What — what?" I asked.

"Your son's in the lake," he panted. "He disappeared."

My mind went blank. Finally my feet found the ability to move. I dashed to the lake, shooting questions as I ran.

"We saw Shannon jumping up and down in the lake," the boy explained. "It sounded like he was saying help, but we thought he was playing."

I ran straight into the lake. Sharp rocks cut into my feet. The water felt like glue, holding me back from my goal.

I launched my body over the lake and began swimming its shallow depths toward where the kid had pointed.

A Wonderful Life

My two older boys had walked through the lake to the other side, where they'd encouraged Shannon to join them. When they saw me, they swam toward me. Within minutes, the chill dragged on Shane, and Shaun had to help him back to shore.

I probed the shallow bottom with hands and feet. Suddenly the lake bottom dropped out from under my feet. *What is this?* I thought as dread gripped me. *Everybody knows Frog Lake is knee deep at the most.*

When I came up for air, I shoved my feet as deep as I could and felt nothing. *No bottom. No son.* An eternity later, my toes grazed something soft.

"Over here!" I hollered at Shaun, who'd taken Shane in and was returning.

We brought Shannon to the surface together. I looked into his eyes.

Lord God, we need you now. I began dragging my son to shore. Exhaustion and hypothermia threatened. *If I don't get hold of something quick, I'm going down, too.*

"Get a boat out there!" I heard someone shout.

"Please, God," I prayed as my strength ebbed, "I don't want to have to let him go."

Someone paddled a canoe out to where I struggled. I slung a numb arm over the edge and hung on. The crowd exploded into action the moment we reached the shore. One began CPR. Another called the emergency squad.

"If you kids believe in God, this is a good time to pray for my son!" I yelled at the stunned boys gathered around us.

Voices from the Valley

Soon, we heard the *thwap, thwap, thwap* of an approaching helicopter. It transported Shannon to the local hospital where the doctor recommended he be transferred to Pediatric ICU at Emanuel Hospital in Portland.

I accompanied my son while Shaun and Shane raced home to break the news to Cindy. A friend drove her the 80 miles to Portland, and she joined me at our son's bedside.

Cindy sang softly to Shannon, over the *hum-plop* of the life-support machinery, while rubbing lotion into his feet. Then she moved to where I stood and slipped her hand into mine.

"We need to pray." I nodded.

"Lord," I began, "he's yours."

"We'd like to keep him," Cindy added, "but if you want him, he's yours."

I looked at my motionless son. "Either heal him 100 percent, Lord, or take him home to you."

The hospital ran tests, and then the doctor called us in for a private conference.

"I'm sorry, Mr. and Mrs. Rovig," he said, "but your son is brain dead." He paused. "We need to remove the life support."

We nodded. That was all we could do.

While friends took our other boys to church and then out to celebrate Shaun's 18th birthday, we released our youngest son to fly home to Jesus.

"I knew he was gone the moment I pulled him to the

A Wonderful Life

surface," I confessed to Cindy. "I looked into his eyes, and I knew."

Cindy squeezed my hand again. "We dedicated him to God at birth," she said. Then she added, "Sweetheart, I never told anyone this before, but somehow I always knew in my heart that our time with him would be short."

☙☙☙

I cradled the funeral bulletin in my hands. Its cover showed a picture Shannon had recently drawn for his great-grandma, with the words *God Made a Wonderful Life* printed on the bottom. I studied the picture and the verses we'd chosen to celebrate his homecoming.

"We believe that Jesus died and rose again and so we believe that God will bring with Jesus those who have fallen asleep in him" (1 Thessalonians 4:14).

You're more alive now, son, than you were on earth. My heart lightened a smidge. *You're probably collecting cans with Jesus now and handing out heavenly candy bars.*

A tear threatened at the memory of a past I'd not enjoy again on earth. I read the next verse. "He will wipe every tear from their eyes. There will be no more death or mourning or crying or pain, for the old order of things has passed away" (Revelation 21:4).

Lord, I thank you for the 12 years you gave us with such an incredible son, and I yield him to you now. I wondered what the rest of my future held for me and recalled the words John McCarty spoke to me so long ago.

Voices from the Valley

You will be greatly used by God, but you will have to endure great hardship first. I bowed my head. *I give whatever is left of my life to you, God.*

Four and a half months later, a man in the church approached me.

"Marlyn," he said, "how would you like to start the jail ministry together in Hood River?"

"If it has anything to do with sharing Jesus and helping men who've lost their way, then I'm all in," I replied.

❧❧❧

Another decade passed. God blessed us with two grandchildren. Even though we liked our church, we felt it had grown too large for our preference and decided to visit River of Life Assembly, where many of our oldest friends attended.

The moment we walked in the door, we sensed the intimacy of a smaller congregation and Pastor Terry's passion for taking the good news of Jesus Christ outside the walls of a church building.

"What good is the church," he preached, "if we confine ourselves to the security and comfort of these four walls? Take Jesus to your neighbors and co-workers. Tell them how he can change their lives, and give them real hope."

I've shared that same passion since Shannon's death, eager to get into jails and talk to embittered, lost and angry men.

I go to an assigned room, where some of the inmates

A Wonderful Life

have gathered and are sitting down. I like to be on the same level as the men, so I sit down, too. I look around at the guys, so despised by themselves and others, so loved by God.

"Okay, guys," I say, "before we get started, I only ask that you come for the right reason — to learn about God and to respect one another. Any questions?"

A few cross their arms. Some grunt. But all remain silent.

"It's open table, guys." I smile to encourage them. "What do you want to discuss today?"

"How do you know there is a God?" one hollers from the back. "We all came from apes."

"Yeah," another agrees, "just look how people act."

"Bible's just a bunch of fairytales," another grouses.

I smile again.

"Good topic," I begin and start laying out detailed answers to address scientific evidence of creation versus evolution.

God helps me take anything that's thrown at me, and I make sure that every conversation gets around to Jesus, the Savior of the world. By the time I leave, the guys know why Jesus came to this earth and are offered the chance to repent and know him personally.

"If God's so loving," another challenges, "why do bad things happen to good people?"

"That's right," another yells. "My sister was raped, and what did she do to deserve that?"

"Where was God then?" a third chimes in.

Voices from the Valley

"Good questions." I hold my hand up for silence. "I've asked the same myself, and I know your pain. Trust me, I do."

Each week, I return to the River of Life Assembly, where freedom of worship and Pastor Terry's challenging messages recharge my spiritual batteries. I take that recharge into the jail and deliver it, like a tall, lanky "carrier pigeon" from God to inmate.

❧ ❧ ❧

When my son Shannon was in elementary school, he presented me with a springtime drawing in black pen on cream paper, which I have kept to this day. Several clouds grace the sky with two birds flying past them. A gabled three-window Hansel and Gretel-style house rests peacefully on a hillside with smoke rising gently from its chimney. A black car is parked in the driveway, and several small people are on the hill next to the house. A lane winds in a half-moon shape from the driveway to disappear behind two trees behind the house. Next to the house, a fisherman boating on a pond holds his rod that bends toward a splashing fish in the water. There is another passenger in the boat looking on.

At the top right of the page, he wrote and underlined these words: "God made a wonderful life."

My boy is right. God did make a wonderful life.

Healing Words
The Story of Amy Hawk
Written by Marty Minchin

I spent a year on my knees, huddled in front of a tiny computer.

The phone rarely rang, and no one knocked on the door of our rented townhouse. My calendar was empty. When Steve walked down to our basement to work and the kids left for school, I retreated upstairs to our bedroom, stepping through the layers of papers and study materials piled up on the floor. I carved out a space in front of my laptop, and the words poured out.

Steve and I had left behind a full, busy life in Spokane. We sold everything and moved to tiny Hood River, Oregon, where we'd vacationed each of our 16 years of marriage. Steve loved to windsurf and relax in the spectacular scenery of the Columbia River Gorge, but we'd never considered living here until now.

It was almost as if I had walked into my destiny because it was so deafeningly quiet that I had nothing to do but write. So I did, and what started as a plan to tell my story in a thousand words or so turned into three books totaling almost 250 pages. I kneeled in front of my tiny computer for hours and days at a time, and I have the veins on my legs to show for it.

My story is about a miracle. My books are about how that miracle could happen to anyone.

Voices from the Valley

☙☙☙

I recognized Steve immediately the night he stepped into a country and western bar in Spokane. He'd only grown more handsome during the past few years, and I hoped he'd remember me. We'd met in junior high, but lost track of each other when we attended different high schools. Now, several years later, we still found each other attractive. He walked over to say hi, and in no time, we were dancing. At the end of the night he walked me out to my car to make sure I made it safely through the parking lot.

The next day Steve came to visit me, and we began dating — and partying — immediately. PJ, Steve's best friend and soccer teammate from high school, had just begun seeing a girl named Jenny, and the four of us became inseparable.

In the summer, we went to PJ's cabin, where we would play games, drink, swim and water ski. In the winter, we would go to bars, drink and dance. We celebrated birthdays, anniversaries and holidays together, and we became engaged at the same time and got married within weeks of each other.

Our wedding could have rivaled those of royalty. For the ceremony, we chose St. John's Cathedral in Spokane, a majestic Episcopal church that looked like a castle with its vaulted ceilings and stone walls. We weren't religious at all; in fact, I wasn't sure I even believed in God. However, I wanted a beautiful wedding, and this church provided a

Healing Words

gorgeous backdrop. Plus, in case there was a God, I wanted to cover all my bases.

We asked my cousin's husband, David, to officiate. We didn't go to church ourselves, and we needed an Episcopal priest to marry us. David was family, and we had hung out with him a few times at reunions at our family cabin. We didn't talk to him much about the wedding beforehand, however, and he arrived from Boise just in time for the rehearsal dinner.

I felt like a princess walking down the long aisle of St. John's, the heavy train of my dress trailing behind me. The lights were dimmed, and candles around the church created a soft, gentle glow. I faced Steve as David began his short talk during the sermon. We had no idea what he planned to say.

David's booming voice echoed through the cathedral.

"This is a couple with passion!" he pronounced. I felt a slight flush in my cheeks as I glanced over at my parents and grandparents sitting in the pews. The elderly lady on the front row, who the church had assigned to direct our ceremony, was frowning.

"This is a couple with passion for life!" David continued, his words surely reaching every corner of the church. "This couple has passion for each other!"

He's getting really personal! At that time, the word passion meant sex, and while Steve and I indeed were passionate that way, we were shocked that David would talk about passion, well, so passionately, at such a formal church service.

Voices from the Valley

We looked at the floor, smiled and blushed while David continued his fiery sermon, and then we walked down the aisle through a sea of smiling guests. Even if they had wanted to clap, the church rules restricted applause in the church sanctuary.

৵৵৵

Steve and I moved into a three-bedroom, three-bathroom house in Spokane. He had earned degrees in math, physics and engineering and landed a good job as a structural engineer. We drove decent cars — I had a Honda Accord, and he drove a Subaru. We'd both grown up in privileged families, and we were used to having nice things. My thoughts were occupied with wondering when he'd get his next promotion and how much he'd be earning.

One day, Steve walked in the door after work and happily told me he'd given $50 to someone in his office whose baby needed medical help. I lost it.

"How could you give our money away?" I yelled, already mourning the nice outfit I could have bought with $50. Even though Steve brought home a good salary, I was always planning ahead for the next nicest house and the next nicest car we would buy when he got a raise.

Our friendship with Jenny and PJ only strengthened after our weddings, and the four of us hit the bars on the weekends as often as we could.

Nothing could have shocked Steve and me more than

Healing Words

when Jenny and PJ asked us to go to church with them.

I grew up in Spokane with my mom, stepdad and sisters, and we never attended church. I had only heard about Jesus Christ at Christmastime, and I put him in the same category as Santa Claus. Steve and I were partiers, not churchgoers, and attending church — especially with our partier friends — seemed completely out of character for all of us. We lived a comfortable life, full of material things. Why in the world would we need Jesus?

Jenny and PJ were the last people we ever expected to go to church, but they started attending one. When they invited us to join them, I wasn't on board with the idea, but Steve wanted to be polite to his friend. I begrudgingly agreed to go a couple of times.

Our friends had already started going to small group Bible studies each week at the church, and I was invited to Jenny's group. I had just had a baby, and the idea of two hours of free babysitting — even if I had to sit through a Bible study for it — was very appealing. I had quit my job after the baby was born, too, so I craved adult interaction.

I wanted to make myself clear to this Bible study group from the start. The first day I walked in, six women looked up at me from their seats around a conference table at the church.

"I'm just here to get a break from the baby," I announced before I even introduced myself. "I don't believe in the Bible, and I'm definitely not buying one."

No one said anything in reply, and I took a seat at the table. They still laugh about it to this day.

Voices from the Valley

❧❧❧

Steve was as lukewarm as I was about church. He was willing to go to the meetings, but neither of us was convinced that the Bible was true. Then, someone in the men's Bible study group that Steve attended with PJ challenged him to read a book called *The Case for Christ* by Lee Strobel. The author's intellectual approach to asking experts about the truth and reliability of the Bible appealed to Steve.

One day, he told me he had decided Jesus was real.

I couldn't believe it. Before Steve read that book, I thought the stories of Jesus Christ dying and rising from the dead were myths. But I trusted my husband, and I knew that if he had done the research and thought it through, he must be right. His pronouncement changed my whole perception of God.

Soon after, I attended a women's conference in Spokane with my Bible study group. At that meeting, I decided that I wanted to dedicate my life to following God. It wasn't a dramatic decision, though, more like an agreement to try out getting to know Jesus. Standing among thousands of women who had made the same choice I had and who were eager to dedicate their lives to following God made my faith in God stronger.

Steve had given me a Bible with my name engraved on it for Christmas the year before. Shannon, my Bible study leader, was guiding us through a very basic study that required us to look up verses in the Bible that talked about

Healing Words

different names for God. My curiosity was piqued, so I started reading the Bible on my own.

Something clicked for Steve and me, and our waffling over whether we truly wanted to follow God ended. Once it really hit us that Christ did die and came back to life, that those events were *real*, our whole perspective on life and how we lived it changed. We went from zero to 100 in terms of our relationship with God, and once we decided we were following God, we followed hard. We wanted to serve Jesus and get involved in the church, and we started leading Bible studies. I couldn't stop reading the Bible. Verses that never made sense to me before suddenly came alive. I started to understand our pastor's sermons. We shared an intense desire to tell our families about God. I even got a job at the church.

Steve and I still wanted to be social, although going out was limited as our family grew to include two children. Instead of partying at bars, we met in people's houses for dinners and lunch. We got to know people at the church, and our friendships deepened with Jenny and PJ, who now had a baby, too, and had decided they wanted God in their lives.

❧❧❧

Throughout my marriage, I was plagued with neck and back pain that stemmed from a car crash I was in just before Steve and I got married. I had visited him overnight at Washington State University in Pullman, where he was

Voices from the Valley

in school, and I left at 5 a.m. for work at a Spokane radio station where I sold advertising. As I drove through downtown Spokane, a woman ran a light, and I hit her.

The airbag burst in front of me, burning my face and chest. She hadn't yielded before she made an unprotected turn, and I slammed into the side of her car.

I wasn't even in the hospital a full day, but the pain that resulted was almost unbearable. It came and went over the months, and nothing I tried — medication, chiropractic care, physical therapy or Cortisone shots — made much of a difference. The pain was at its worst at the end of the day, and some days Steve would come home from work and find me curled up on the floor in a fetal position trying to relieve the pain in my back.

My pregnancies with my two children only intensified the pain. Carrying them around as babies and toddlers made it so much worse, and doctors finally recommended surgery. We had two young children, and our health insurance coverage through Steve's job recently had changed. Surgery would be too expensive and painful, and I resigned myself to a life spent in pain.

Surgery, it turned out, wasn't my only option. A friend at church mentioned the Healing Room in downtown Spokane, and my life changed forever.

అఅఅ

The lady from church gave me a book by John G. Lake about his healing ministries, which he founded in the early

Healing Words

1900s. I read through the book, but his ideas about physical healing didn't match up with what my church taught. Lake believed that Jesus healed people physically in the Bible and wants people to be physically healed that way today. Leaders at my church believed that healing was only for some people. God, they said, sometimes preferred that you be patient with pain instead of being healed.

Needless to say, I was skeptical about the Healing Room, but since there was a ministry in downtown Spokane, I thought I would give it a try.

I was nervous to go, but it seemed like everywhere I turned, people were talking about it. I'd hear about the Healing Room in a passing conversation, or people would mention it to me in an offhand way. As a safeguard, I took Steve with me. He's very smart, and if he detected any funny business, we'd leave right away.

We pulled up in front of a nondescript white building in a rough area of downtown Spokane. We had to look twice to make sure we had the right place. From the plain exterior, you'd never guess the building was where people went looking for miracles.

The lobby looked just like a doctor's office. Several people sat in chairs around the edge of the room, laughing and chatting. I signed in at the front desk — the Healing Room didn't take appointments — and wrote "neck and back pain" on a sticky note so volunteers would know what I wanted them to pray for. The receptionist asked me to fill out a standard health form, which asked whether I followed God and for a description about why I was there.

Voices from the Valley

At the bottom, I signed to acknowledge that I was not there for counseling or to seek medical help.

The atmosphere in the room was unlike any lobby I'd ever sat in. I didn't feel weird or uneasy or feel the heavy air of uncertainty that so often permeates a doctor's waiting area. Some people had brought their friends, and I could sense their faith and hopefulness. Peace settled in the room, and I knew that God was there.

This is okay, I thought. *There's nothing wrong with prayer. This is worth checking out.*

After about 20 minutes, a volunteer called my name.

She led Steve and me into a room, where we met the three people who would pray for us. They looked like a sweet grandma and grandpa and a nice lady, all people we couldn't possibly be afraid of. We were surprised when they announced that they felt led to talk to God about our marriage first, not my back and neck.

We stood up and bowed our heads, and the prayer volunteers' words flowed around us. My ears perked up when they talked about our marriage being infused with passion. Eleven years before, we had heard those same words at our wedding. We hadn't talked about our priest's fiery wedding sermon in more than 10 years, but when the prayer volunteers said the word *passion*, it came flooding back.

The prayer volunteers spoke as if they were in direct communication with God.

"God says he has bestowed passion on you, passion in unity, passion in every aspect of your life."

Healing Words

I gripped Steve's hand, and we looked at each other, smiling and laughing at what we took to be a sure sign that God knew us. The prayer volunteers were using the exact phrases as the priest at our wedding.

"There is an umbrella of passion for everything you do. You have a passion for Jesus."

Only God could have caused such an uncanny connection. How else would these volunteers, who we'd never seen before in our lives, know what had been said at our wedding? Their words were almost verbatim to the priest's blessing.

I believed without a doubt that God was there in the room with us. He was sending us a message through the volunteers' prayers.

God was at our wedding, I realized, *even though God wasn't part of my life then. He knew us, even though we didn't know him. He brought Steve and me together, and he's been watching over us.*

The volunteers finally asked about my neck and back, and I recounted the story of the car crash and my years of pain. I felt comfortable when they dabbed a tiny spot of oil on my forehead and laid their hands on me as they began to talk to God about my pain. One man set his hands on the back of my neck, and a rush of heat flooded through me. I twisted my neck a little to see if I could detect a heating pad there, but I felt nothing other than his hands.

I finally asked him, "What do you have on the back of my neck?"

"Just my hands," he replied.

Voices from the Valley

The prayer thrilled me, but I honestly did not expect that my pain would go away. As I stepped into the parking lot afterward, however, my back seemed to feel better. On the way to the car, I told Steve I thought I'd been healed.

❧❧❧

The pain disappeared.

I suddenly could cope with my life and my kids, and I no longer was impatient and grumpy. Unloading the dishwasher without pain was reason to rejoice. One day, to test my healing, I didn't wake up my 4 year old after he fell asleep in the car. Before the healing prayer, I couldn't have carried him inside when we got home. This time I carefully unbuckled him, lifted him out of his car seat and carried him up a flight of stairs to his bed. I felt no pain, not even a twinge. I was a whole new person with a whole new back.

My healing set my relationship with God on fire. Steve and I were incredulous about this miracle, and I was drawn back to the Healing Room over and over for more prayer. The people there, I believed, knew God better than I did, and I wanted what they had.

Random people prayed for me at the Healing Room, volunteers I had never seen before.

I would read a verse in the Bible at home in the morning, and in the afternoon a Healing Room volunteer would say the same verse during our prayer session. The Healing Room was opening up a whole world of spiritual

Healing Words

power and activity I had never heard about in church.

The pages of my Bible just seemed to flip open to verses about physical healing every time I studied it. It dawned on me that God was trying to speak to me through the Bible and teach me about how he heals people's bodies. I began scribbling down the Bible verses on a set of note cards on a wire ring, and in no time I had 50 cards filled, and I hadn't even read through half the Bible yet. I knew that God wanted me to understand that he cares about healing people.

I read every book about physical healing that I could get my hands on. When I learned that the Healing Room offered a training course for potential prayer volunteers, I signed up immediately. I began volunteering there every other Saturday.

I was bursting to tell anyone and everyone that God healed my back and couldn't wait to share my story at my church's monthly staff meeting. Each meeting's agenda included a time when staff members and pastors could share what God had been doing in their lives, and I told them the whole story about God healing my back pain. You could hear a pin drop in the room when I finished, and I flushed when I realized that they were skeptical.

I'm so embarrassed, God. I'm not going to tell my story anymore.

But by the time I got home, I decided God had healed me so that I could tell people about the amazing thing he had done.

I'm not going to be ashamed or disgraced.

Voices from the Valley

My confidence surged. I felt I'd tapped into a world of spiritual battles, that God and Satan were fighting for me in a realm I'd never sensed before. I now believed that the devil tries to squelch God's work in the world. I was sure that God had healed me, and now nobody was going to shut me up.

I walked confidently into my pastor's office a few days later to talk to him further about my healing. We did not agree on every point of doctrine about healing, but he let me start a new healing ministry at our church.

My training from the Healing Room got a workout. In my healing ministry for the church, which I modeled after the Healing Room, I prayed for headaches, anxiety, cancer, anything you can think of. I began to understand that oftentimes people would come in with physical problems, but after listening to God, I saw that the root of their problem was anxiety, depression or another emotional problem. After they wrote their ailment on a piece of paper, I would talk to God about it. Then I would sit quietly, waiting for God to respond by bringing words and ideas into my mind and heart. I would ask God what my volunteers and I should say to the person. Many times, it was completely unrelated to what they said they wanted us to pray about. They'd often cry in response, touched by how much God loved them because he had shown the prayer volunteers something else about their lives.

❦❦❦

Healing Words

A few years later, a mole on my back began to itch. It was a little difficult to reach and hard for me to see in a mirror. I had never noticed it before because it was so tiny. Steve looked at it and suggested I call my doctor.

The doctor said the mole appeared harmless, but he removed it and sent it to a lab for testing, as a precaution. Two days before Christmas of 2009, our phone rang. The doctor said it was cancer.

I was shocked. The lab had to be wrong. There's no way I could have cancer.

"We've sent the mole to two different labs," he said. "They confirmed that it's cancer."

I could hear my kids moving around in the family room next to the kitchen, and I fought to keep my voice flat so they couldn't hear my panic. If I cried, they'd know something was wrong.

"You need to get to the oncologist immediately," the doctor went on. "I've already called one I've worked with before. She has your records, and she's expecting your call."

Earlier that morning, Steve had found an old note card of mine stuck under a cabinet. I had written on it, "I did not give you a spirit of fear," a phrase from the Bible verse 1 Timothy 1:7 that I'd copied during my frenzied reading about physical healing. I held the worn paper in my hand and stared at it as the doctor talked, his voice slurring into a drone as my thoughts crystallized, obscuring his words.

Do not fear.
This is a set-up from the devil.

Voices from the Valley

God wants me to be healed 100 percent.

By the time I hung up the phone, I was furious. And I wanted to laugh.

Satan, you picked the wrong person to mess with. I can believe God's word, or I can believe this diagnosis. I am going to live. This spiritual battle is ON.

❧❧❧

The call came in the middle of our hectic preparations for a family ski trip. We planned to celebrate Christmas Day at home and leave for Silver Mountain the next day. We had booked a condo with my mom and my three sisters and their families. Getting ready to go had completely absorbed me, and I knew the trip would be a wonderful time with my family.

I checked in with a nurse the next day, and she told me to cancel the vacation.

"You need to come in right away." Her words echoed the doctor from the day before. "This is type four melanoma, nothing to mess around with. The cancer has been there a couple of months, and it could get into your bloodstream. This can't wait."

I decided it could wait. After praying about whether I should call off the vacation and discussing it with Steve, I was convinced that Satan was trying to scare me. I told my doctor I was going skiing, and I made an appointment for the day after we planned to return. My children were looking forward to spending time with their cousins. My

Healing Words

stepfather had died of cancer in 2006, and Christmas already was an emotional time for my mom. The last thing I wanted to do was call my mom and tell her I had cancer, especially at Christmastime.

So we skied, and I kept my secret.

The cancer stayed on my mind that week, as if Satan was prodding me with fear whenever he could. On an outing to an indoor water park, I picked up a magazine while the kids swam, and I flipped right to a huge article about a celebrity and how her brother had died of skin cancer. The guy had to be my age or younger. Other times, the chaos of the kids and food and fun kept me distracted. I refused to let the diagnosis dampen my mood.

At the oncologist's office later that week, the doctor delivered some surprising news. I had assumed she would just remove a little more skin from around the mole, test it and report back that the skin was cancer-free and I was fine. However, she told us the cancer was the type that spreads to your blood, and she would not be content testing only a little skin from my back.

"There could be cancer cells a quarter inch away," she explained. "Sometimes this cancer can spread rapidly. We're looking at extensive surgery."

She wanted to remove more skin around the mole, another mole on my foot and two lymph nodes from under my arm. I was completely against the surgery, certain that God would heal me. This was a much bigger deal than I anticipated, and I didn't want to have anything to do with it. Steve urged me to have the surgery, however, so reluctantly I agreed. We set the date for January 23, three weeks away, and then embarked on a fast, where we limited what we ate to just a few foods. This helped us focus our minds on God so that we could better understand what he wanted. Steve and I needed unity on how to proceed.

During our fasting and prayer, a Bible verse came to Steve's mind from the book of Isaiah: "Though you search for your enemies, you will not find them." I clearly understood then what God wanted us to know. God wanted me to go through the surgery, because when the doctors found no cancer, I could tell everyone my story and show people that God was amazing because he healed me and answered our prayers. There was no doubt in my mind that tests on my mole, skin and lymph nodes would show no cancer.

I opened up to my friends, my family and my church about my cancer. Leaders in our church prayed for me, and I made many trips to the Healing Room. I knew I was healed before I walked into that operating room.

❧❧❧

The surgeon removed a diamond-shaped patch of skin from my back and then stitched it up. I could hardly walk on the foot where the mole had been removed, so I was resigned to lying in bed with my foot propped up for a week. That's how long it took for the nurse to call me with the results of the tests.

Healing Words

"Congratulations." Her voice didn't sound very congratulatory. She read the results like a judge reads a list of jury verdicts. "They did not find any cancer on your back. They did not find any cancer on your foot. There was no cancer in your lymph nodes."

My heart leaped.

Just before the phone rang, I had been reading the book of Isaiah in my Bible. I wrote down a verse describing a group of people who got good news, celebrated with joy and told everyone they could about it.

"It happens sometimes," the nurse went on. "There's no cancer. It looks like you got lucky this time. We'll see you in a week for your checkup."

I dialed Steve and told him about the verse in Isaiah and the nurse's call. We cried with relief, knowing that the cancer scare was behind us. I was healed!

It was time for me to tell the nations my own good news. I composed an e-mail about my experience and sent it to my pastors, my friends and family. All of the credit, I wrote, went to God.

ಸಿಸಿಸಿ

I have told my story to anyone who would listen, and in Spokane, that was a lot of people. We were always busy, hanging out with friends or going to church every time the doors were opened. The phone rarely stopped ringing.

But God had more in mind. God kept impressing on us that we needed to move, although we weren't sure where or why. Steve and I blindly obeyed. God told us to sell everything we had and give the money to the poor, and we believed God was preparing us to be missionaries in another country. We were ready and eager to go wherever God directed us.

First, we had to get rid of the mass of stuff we had accumulated over the years. All we planned to keep were our clothes and the mattresses off the beds.

On the day of our big yard sale, most of our material possessions were spread out over our front lawn and driveway — our three couches, our bed frames, our kitchen utensils and our linens. Cars and cars of people came by, and I felt a strange contentment all day as they carried off my worldly goods. What we didn't sell, we gave away. Only my beautiful Ethan Allen dining table, which could seat 12 with leaves inserted, was hard to part with. I knew, however, that we wouldn't have room for it in our new lives. I gave it to a friend at church who was thrilled to own such a large table.

We donated all of the proceeds to a women's shelter.

Our missionary assignment turned out to be a little closer to home. Steve and I believed that God was telling us to move to Hood River, a small town where we frequently had vacationed but never considered moving to.

Saying goodbye to dear friends, including Jenny and PJ and their kids, was the hardest part of leaving Spokane. In Hood River, we moved our mattresses and suitcases into a little condominium. Unlike the first time Steve and I

Healing Words

moved, I didn't care where we lived. I didn't need a giant house and beautiful clothes to feel like a princess. I felt special because God had confirmed to us that we were living the life he wanted us to. We may not have been in an exotic foreign country working as missionaries, but we knew whatever we'd be doing in Hood River would be just as important.

༄༄༄

Our busy social lives came to a screeching halt in Hood River. Suddenly, our calendar was empty. In those first few months, our phone was silent.

But the space and time in Hood River freed me to write. We were so busy in Spokane that I never would have taken the time there to put my story on the page.

After two years, we have decided to put down roots in Hood River. Steve's job has let him work remotely, so he has established a home office here. We just moved into a little house behind our children's school, which the kids love. We have made some friends and enjoyed visits from loved ones in Spokane, including Jenny and PJ.

I pray for people any opportunity I get. After services at River of Life, our new church, we stand in the front and pray for anyone who comes up. I visit people's houses to talk and pray, and many have been physically healed.

This fall, a friend is opening a Healing Room in the Columbia River Gorge area. Because of my training from Spokane, I am already on the roster as a prayer volunteer.

Voices from the Valley

In the Bible, there are many stories about Jesus healing people's bodies, and I know that Jesus is willing to do the same for people today. When hurting people walk through those doors, I will be there to pray with confidence that God will make them well. Physical healing is a central part of Jesus' life and story — and mine.

Fearless Forgiveness
The Story of Janelle
Written by Laura Florio

My hands lightly grazed the polished wood of the chairs, worn from years of use but still gleaming, as my eyes approached the bench where the judge was seated. Behind me, my parents and my sister sat with hands clenched tightly together and bated breath. The judge gave me a cursory smile and motioned for me to come forward. I somehow managed to pull myself into a standing position and forced my feet to move in his direction. The attorney placed his hand on my shoulder to brace me. "Is there anything you would like to add before I pronounce the verdict?"

"No, Your Honor," I murmured. My gaze plunged to my shoes and the floor tiles. The paperclip I had been toying with throughout the hearing was now completely destroyed. The judge looked over his bifocals to eye the rest of the people gathered in the California courtroom.

"I have reached a verdict. I pronounce Zek Amnon guilty on the charges of armed robbery, unlawful use of a weapon, rape and attempted sexual assault and sentence him to seven years in the California State Prison. Mr. Amnon has been made aware of his sentence, as well as the other victim, Carol." The decisive crack of the gavel reverberated through the room. "Court is adjourned!"

With that, the judge rose and briskly made his exit to

his chambers. The rush of relief manifested itself in tears as I felt my father's arm wrapped securely around me and my mother's hand gently stroking my face. I fell into my family's arms. "You did good, honey," my father whispered reassuringly into my hair. "Real good."

"Oh, darling, I am so proud of you," my mom said through a veil of tears. "Justice has been served to that horrible man, and now we can all go home and put this as far away from you as possible. Come on. Let's get you out of here. Doug will meet with you later this afternoon."

Leaning on my father for support, my family escorted me out of the courtroom and into the car. The day was crisp and clear, but it felt foggy and rainy inside my soul.

Previously, the police led me into one of the small offices at the back of the station. "Ma'am, in order to make sure this guy goes to jail for a very long time, we're going to need you to identify him."

I gulped. "But I don't ever want to look him in the eye again. How can I … after what he did?"

"Ma'am," the officer looked deep into my eyes, "I understand this must be difficult for you, especially you being 17 and all, but we all want this guy off the streets and as far away from you as possible. I am not asking you to face him. There will be a wall of glass, and he will not be able to see you. My partner and I will be standing beside you the entire time, and your parents will be waiting outside the door. We just need to make sure we're going to put the right guy away. Otherwise, he goes free and might try what he did to you again on some other poor girl."

Fearless Forgiveness

I let out a long breath. "If you can promise me I will never have to see him again after this …"

"I promise!" The young officer looked like he meant it with all of his heart.

"Okay."

I still remember the walk from the office to the room where I would identify my attacker. During what seemed an eternity, my feet felt more and more like concrete blocks the closer we came to the room. My arms folded tightly across my chest, I approached the window. A buzzer went off, a door opened on the other side of the glass and a line of straggly looking men shuffled across the room. My eyelids squinted tightly together as I tried to shield myself from the nauseating wave of memories that overcame me, and I bowed my head as soon as his face came into view. He stood staring out into space, seemingly disengaged with his surroundings and unconcerned about his fate. "That's him." I pointed and continued to look away.

"You sure?"

"More than I have ever been."

"Good. We are going to do our best to make sure you never lay eyes on him again." The officer's partner quickly escorted me out of the room and into my parents' comforting embrace.

❧❧❧

Voices from the Valley

"Come on, Dad," Carol pleaded. "It will be fine! Look, it doesn't even get dark until 8:45, anyway. It's kind of quiet tonight. Go home, please, and enjoy an evening with Mom for once instead of rushing to get back here to close."

Her father, Mr. Saunders, sighed. "And you'll remember to lock the back door? And take all the money out from the cash register early, okay?"

"Yes, yes and yes to everything else you want to ask me to do. I've been in this store since I was an infant. But I'm not a baby anymore. I am 24 years old, and I know this place like the back of my hand, and I promise to take very good care of it."

Mr. Saunders sighed again, but this time he smiled. "Okay, okay, fine. You can close tonight. I will be by the phone if you need anything. Just call, alright?"

Carol squealed with delight, winked at me and hugged her father. "Thank you, thank you, thank you! I promise you won't be disappointed!" Mr. Saunders laughed, picked up his briefcase and walked down the street to his car. Carol and I looked at each other and giggled. "Freedom!" she proclaimed and high-fived me.

Summertime was taking a bow, and I was about to begin my senior year of high school. The world lay before me like the promise of adventure, and I planned to seize every moment of it. I had gotten this job at the retail shop two years before. My grandmother worked five stores down and knew the owners, Mr. and Mrs. Saunders. My parents allowed me to work during the summers and on

Fearless Forgiveness

weekends, provided that I gave 10 percent to my church and saved another 10 percent. I could do what I wished with the rest. I did not take the financial responsibility lightly. I recorded all my earnings and purchases in a blue flip-spiral notebook.

For me, it was a dream job. Rows of bulk candy lined the store, along with a popcorn machine and trinkets that Mr. Saunders purchased from Mexico. The goodies attracted many of my high school friends and church pals. Mr. Saunders was a gentle but disciplined boss, and his daughter, Carol, often worked with me. That night was the first time Mr. Saunders ever allowed Carol to close. Normally, he worked during the day, drove home for dinner and then returned to close around 8:30 p.m. Carol, home from college, acted as the assistant manager while she applied for jobs outside of the small California town where we lived.

❧❧❧

"Hi, did you find everything you needed?" I asked the man at the counter with a smile.

"Uh, yeah. Actually, can I see your pocket knives?"

"Of course. Is there one in particular that you wanted to look at?"

"No, I want to see which one is the sharpest."

"You've got a camping trip coming up?"

"Yeah, something like that." The man spent a great deal of time mulling over the right blade, but it was fairly

Voices from the Valley

busy that evening, so I helped the other customers while he made his selection. Finally, when there were only a few people left, he chose one. He left it at the front and went back for some strapping tape. He took his time getting up to the register. By this time, no one else was in the store.

"That will be $14.79, please," Carol said as I carefully placed his purchases in a bag and handed it to him.

He gave us this ugly lopsided grin, gingerly took out the knife and said, "Actually, I'm here to rob you. Give me all your money."

The world stopped for a moment. Carol and I glanced at each other briefly before she opened the register and systematically placed the money in a bag. That finished, we both looked up at him, hoping he would leave. There was no security button, and nobody on the street to hear us scream. "Now lock the door. Quickly, before someone comes." Carol took the key, walked slowly to the door and locked it. Her hands shook so much that it proved difficult for her to lock. Finally, it clicked. "Now get in the back," he said, waving the knife toward the rear of the store. Grasping each other's hands, Carol and I shuffled slowly in that direction.

When we arrived in the storage area, he barked, "Now take off all your clothes, even your underwear. And do it quickly before I stab you!" Carol and I shed our garments and then held out our hands while he bound them with the strapping tape. Then he pushed me roughly toward a corner of the storage area where birdcages were kept. With his knife indenting my thigh, he muttered, "On your back,

Fearless Forgiveness

b****, and if you make any noise, I'll kill you." Silently, I laid down and mentally checked out while he batted my legs apart and pushed himself on top of me. Call it survival mechanism, but I felt like I was floating above what was happening. The whole time, in my mind, I heard the words from Psalm 27, which were familiar to me from my upbringing: "The Lord is my light and my salvation. Whom do I fear?" I barely heard Carol screaming in the distance.

"Are you okay? Are you okay?" she called out.

When he was finished, he nudged me to stand up. I groggily got to my feet and followed him back to where Carol was. "What'd you do to her, you b******?" Carol fumed.

"Nothing I ain't going to do to you. Get over here." They tussled all the way to the birdcages. I heard more shoving and grunting, but I was too much in shock to yell or cry out. After a few minutes, they emerged, and he demanded the keys. "Don't even think about following me," he said as he brandished the knife with one final flourish before exiting the front door.

As we heard his footsteps diminish and the sound of the front door being unlocked and opened, Carol turned to me. "Are you okay? Did he hurt you?" I nodded, and tears stung my eyes. "Oh, honey, we have got to get you out of here!" As quietly as we could, we opened the back door, which led to an alley. After peering around to make sure he wasn't there, we grabbed our pants and started running down the street. About a block away, there were

Voices from the Valley

some apartments. Carol and I each picked a door and started banging. "Please help us! Open the door! We've been robbed, and we need to call the police!"

Finally, a woman appeared at the door. "Gracious," she murmured when she saw our taped wrists and naked chests. "Come in, right away. Hurry!" We stumbled into her apartment, and she called for her husband to fetch a few of his work shirts. We donned them, and then she led us into the living room, where we sat while she called the police.

"Yes, Officer, I would like to report an armed robbery and assault. I have the two girls here. Yes, yes, please come as soon as possible. Thank you." When she hung up, she turned to me. "Are your parents JoAnn and Harold?"

"Yes," I replied, surprised to hear my parents' names spoken by a stranger.

"Oh, my! I was in your parents' Sunday school class several years ago. Your mother is a wonderful lady. Thank the Lord we were the ones who opened up the door." She got up and put her arms around me and then reached for the phone. "What's your number, Janelle?"

I whispered my number.

"I am going to call your parents and then Carol's. They must be informed as soon as possible."

Within minutes, everyone descended upon the apartment. At that point, my out-of-body experience ended, and I felt myself plunged into the dreadful reality of the situation at hand. Raised by conservative parents, I believed sex was for marriage. When I saw my mother

Fearless Forgiveness

walk into the room, I broke down and wept. There were very few words exchanged that evening, but there were many hugs. I thanked God we found the refuge of that couple's home. The police allowed me the space to cry and be consoled by my parents. Mr. Saunders arrived looking very haggard. After a brief conversation with Carol, he approached my parents and me.

"I can assure you that we will do everything in our power to make sure Janelle gets the services she needs, no matter the cost. I am so very sorry. I should have never left them alone. I … I can't believe this filthy thing happened in my store. It's almost too much to handle."

My dad rested his arm on Mr. Saunders' shoulder. "We greatly appreciate your help, but we know this was something completely out of your control."

Mr. Saunders glanced down at me. "We are going to get him and make sure he stays in jail for a nice long time."

The policeman strode over to where I was standing. "Ma'am, I am going to have to ask you to come down to the hospital with us. We need to give you a physical to make sure you are all right. Then we will accompany you to the station. We're also going to need a description of this pervert so we can catch him."

I laid my head on my mom's shoulder and nodded weakly. I felt as though someone had crumpled up my insides and thrown them away. My parents gently guided me to the patrol car, and my mom rode with Carol and me.

Voices from the Valley

We arrived at the hospital, were separated and met with a very sympathetic doctor for examinations. After the doctor examined me, I dressed in some clothes that my parents brought and went to the police station, which was abuzz with activity. Word had spread about the robbery and the assault, and orders were being dispatched and police headed in every direction. The officer with us steered us clear of the chaos and into a small office, where a sketch artist waited with a drawing pad and some charcoal.

"Can you describe this guy for me, young lady?" It was amazing to watch my verbal description take two-dimensional shape, but I shuddered when I saw the eyes.

"Yes, that's exactly how he looked," I said.

"Tell me about his clothes. Did he wear anything in particular that stood out to you?"

"Well," I thought for a minute, "I think he wore khaki shorts and a black shirt. And flip flops. I think he had on flip flops. I didn't see any jewelry."

"Okay, I think we've got a good picture. You've been very brave and very helpful today, young lady, and I believe you are going to come out of this just fine. Thank you for all you did to help us get this guy off the streets for good."

"You're welcome, sir."

"Here's my card. Please call me if you think of anything else."

"Yes, sir."

Fearless Forgiveness

֍֍֍

The charcoal drawing was published in a large spread the next day in the paper. It turned out that a postman saw the guy fiddling around in his car, had a bad feeling about him and wrote down his license plate. With that information, the police soon apprehended him. It turned out he was from the nearby town of Oakland, California.

֍֍֍

"How are you feeling today?" Doug, the counselor, peered at me intently. We sat side by side in two oversized comfy chairs in his office. There was a peace in his office that seemed to evade me at home. I felt like I could finally breathe and talk about what I was thinking.

"Honestly, I don't feel anything at the moment. I'm not even angry. I'm, like, numb."

"What's been happening at home?"

"Well, it seems like everyone is feeling something except for me. My dad eats his dinner with clenched hands, and I can hear him whispering angrily to my mom after we all go to bed. My mother has ramped up her nurturing and caters to my every whim. Robby, my boyfriend, is also super-supportive. My sister won't let me out of her sight — actually, no one will. They all hover. My brothers are pretty normal about it because they were at camp when it all happened, and they're young. The kids at school don't know — they all get something's happened, but they don't know it was me. The only people who know, outside of my family, are Mr. Saunders and the youth pastors at my church. And they're also pretty mad about the whole thing. Still," I paused for a moment to gather my thoughts, "there are some great things going on around me. Life is still happening, and I am still breathing. I didn't die, and I'm about to start college. I want to get over this. I want to live my life."

He smiled. "You will. There is a divine plan in place, and I pray when the feelings finally do come, you will be able to deal with the anger without letting it get the best of you."

"You know what? You know what I really think?"

"What?"

"He's in jail right now, and I am free. But something tells me that if I don't forgive him and move on with my life, that I will be the one behind bars."

The counselor looked at me intently. "That's a lot of wisdom for a 17 year old. It seems as if God has given you special help in healing from this violation."

I smiled. "They say I am really lucky. I didn't get pregnant, and I didn't have to spend any time in the same room with him like other girls have had to do in the past. It was really hard to have to pick him out of the line-up, and when the lawyers questioned me, it was horrendous. But knowing he can't hurt anyone else helps a lot, and knowing that God loves me and has the ability to turn this into good encourages me to move past it.

"Since I started to believe in and know Jesus at 7 years old, I felt like he has given me a clear idea of how much he loves me. I also felt as though he somehow protected me in the way described in the Bible: 'Do not fear, for I have redeemed you; I have summoned you by name; you are mine ... when you walk through the fire, you will not be burned; the flames will not set you ablaze. For I am the Lord your God ... your Savior.'

"That's what I think happened to me," I told Doug. "That man tried to 'burn' me by raping me, but I've clung to my hope in God, and God has not allowed him to succeed."

"What you say points to your attitude. I once read a quote that I want to share with you that has helped me to evaluate my attitude during difficult times. I hope that it proves helpful to you on your journey toward healing. It's a quote from the well-known author and pastor Charles Swindoll: 'Attitude is more important than the past, than education, than money, than circumstances, than what other people think or say or do. It is more important than appearance, giftedness or skill. It will make or break a company, a church, a home. The remarkable thing is that we have a choice every day regarding attitude we will embrace for that day. We cannot change the inevitable, the only thing we can do is play on the one string we have, and that is our attitude.'

"I think you have a winning attitude, Janelle, and I pray God uses your attitude to bring strength and healing to others."

Voices from the Valley

❧❧❧

Mr. Saunders provided me with workman's comp for the next six months, and I continued to see Doug once a week. I threw myself into school and violin practice, and the year passed quickly.

In June, I graduated and returned to work. By then, Carol had moved to another town, and both Mr. Saunders and his wife were present whenever I worked. I found out I had been accepted to Southern California College, a small liberal arts Christian college for the fall of 1981. Excited for all the opportunities that the future held, I couldn't wait to start.

❧❧❧

"Excuse me, excuse me," a voice called from the front of the room. "Is there a Janelle in here? I need to talk to her." As a shy person, this was not the sort of attention I sought on the very first day of my college courses. Besides, who was this strange guy asking for me? I had never seen him before. I sunk down in my chair and ignored the plea. "Janelle? Janelle? I really need to talk to you!"

As the guy made his way up my row, I glanced up from the book I was pretending to read and hissed, "Look, I am not sure what you want, but I am positive it can wait until after class."

"I really need to talk with you outside."

"There is no way I am going outside to talk with you."

The fellow groaned and rolled his eyes. "Okay, but at

Fearless Forgiveness

least talk to the band instructor. We really need a violinist." And with that, he walked out.

Sure enough, he was right. The band instructor led a small ensemble called the Vanguards. The group of musicians and singers traveled to various churches to perform and promote our college. Despite my odd initial encounter with the guy, Terry, who ended up being the bass singer for the group, I joined. A month later, Terry asked me out. We dated for two years.

During Easter break, we decided to visit my parents. I had a feeling that he might propose that week, as he wanted to ask my dad's permission to marry me. However, the week came and went without any proposal. The last day before we were to leave, we took a trip with my younger brothers to San Francisco. *Surely, he will find some romantic nook in which to ask me,* I thought to myself as we set off. However, the day passed without incident, and my brothers always seemed to be around at the wrong time. That night, I decided to do laundry.

"Babe, I've got something to ask you," Terry said.

"What is it, love?" I said, look up from folding clothes.

Terry was grinning from ear to ear and held a ring in his hand. "Oh, no, you don't," I said.

"What?" Terry looked crestfallen.

"Absolutely not. We are not doing this here in this laundry room!" I grabbed his free hand and led him into the living room. I shook out my hair, smoothed my clothes and looked at him. "You were saying?"

Terry fell to his knees, relieved to be able to finish his

proposal, offered up the ring and gazed into my eyes. "Janelle, you are the most practical romantic I have ever met in my life. I've loved you since the first day you shafted me in that classroom. You're the one that I love, and I want to spend the rest of our lives together, making music and having adventures. Will you marry me?"

I smiled, clasped his hand and kissed him. "Yes, I will marry you, Terry. I was beginning to think you would never ask."

"Sorry, I've been dying to ask you so many times this week, but I really wanted to get your father's permission first, and we were only able to sit down and have that conversation 10 minutes ago."

"Did it end well?" I teased.

"He gave me his blessing, and you said yes. I can't imagine a more perfect ending than that." Terry smiled and moved in for another kiss.

❧❧❧

Terry and I married that August. We chose a larger Assembly of God church than the church we attended for the ceremony and held our reception at the Methodist church where my dad and brothers worked as part-time janitors. Our parents and friends prepared a lovely sit-down dinner for about 350 guests. Terry wrote and performed a song for me called "You're the One I Love." After the wedding, 100 people accompanied Terry and me back to my parents' house where we opened gifts. I still

Fearless Forgiveness

remember the look on Terry's face when we opened the brass dinner bell. "What are you going to do with that?" he whispered.

"I guess I can use it to call you to dinner when you're out in the fields growing our food," I whispered back.

To this day, we have not used it, but it's gone with us in every move we've made.

☙☙☙

Since Terry decided to study theology and music, with the idea of becoming a pastor, I decided to switch my major from music to business.

We moved from the dorms to married student housing in a trailer park. Our "home" was a 10x40-foot pink and white trailer. To most people it would appear small, but after living in a 10x10-foot dorm room, we thought we were living pretty high. For extra income, Terry quit the Vanguards and started driving a school bus. I followed suit so that we could spend more time together. We were so very much in love.

Terry graduated in 1984 and immediately procured a job as the Minister of Music at a church in Grass Valley, California.

Since Grass Valley was quite a distance away, I decided to leave school, and we packed up our belongings from the tiny trailer and moved into a small rental house.

☙☙☙

Voices from the Valley

"Why so glum?" I asked one evening as Terry walked through the door. He sighed and dropped a kiss on my forehead and gently patted my growing tummy.

"The pastor and I seem to share different philosophies about church music. I've really tried this past year to meet him in the middle, but we simply don't agree. I've been looking around, and I found a job in Oakland, but …"

"Really? In Oakland? Oh, honey, that's so wonderfully close to my parents! And such perfect timing, too, with the little one on the way."

"You think?" Terry's face immediately brightened. "It's just that there's a lapse between jobs. If we leave now, I won't have insurance when the baby comes, nor will I have the income to cover our housing costs."

"Why don't we move in with my parents? They will be over the moon when they find out we have the opportunity to be so close. And I'm sure God will provide something when it comes time for the little one. He always does."

Terry hugged me. "Thanks, Janelle, for understanding. I feel like going to Oakland is an important step."

I embraced him and murmured, "Another step in our great adventure."

As it turned out, the church in Grass Valley graciously agreed to pay Terry's salary for the three months following his resignation, as well as pay for the hospital fees for our little girl, Jennifer, who was born in September of 1985. We packed our belongings, moved them into storage and went to live with my parents, who were indeed thrilled to

Fearless Forgiveness

have their new grandbaby living with them under the same roof. Terry loved the Oakland job, we eventually found a house to rent and our little family flourished. In 1987, we welcomed our second daughter, Jamie, into the world. With extra mouths to feed, I began teaching piano lessons. Between my piano teaching and Terry's choir performances, music became a permanent part of our home. Terry and I also ran a summer music camp where we taught and performed an entire musical to the kids attending in one week. Our son, Jeremy, was born in 1989, and we felt the seams of the house stretch to fit us.

☙☙☙

"Hello, darling," I greeted Terry as he practically waltzed in the door. "You look happy."

"I am quite happy, actually. I received a call from a church in Albany, Oregon, today. They have a burgeoning music program with a decent choir *and* an orchestra. They seem to think I would be a perfect fit for their music program, and so I was wondering if I could have the pleasure of your company for a little jaunt to Oregon?"

"Well, a choir with an orchestra does sound pretty amazing. I could play violin again …"

"Indeed, and they provide an additional housing supplement. With the extra money, we could — "

" — buy a house?!" I finished the phrase for him. "Oh, Terry, that would be so great. I've always dreamed of our children having a proper backyard."

Voices from the Valley

"So you would be willing to go for a visit?"

"Yes. I think my parents could watch the children for a few days. And we really have outgrown this house."

So in 1990, our family moved to Albany, Oregon. We found a ranch home with a huge lot near the church and settled in.

The house was actually once a pot house, so we had to renovate everything, from the floors to the windows to the walls to the electrical outlets. But after a lot of work and a complete overhaul, it felt like home.

The choir blossomed to more than 100 people under Terry's leadership, and I enjoyed my time playing violin in the orchestra.

Eventually, I started a hand bell choir, and Terry and I put together an Independence Day musical, complete with fireworks and a picnic in the park. Our family also took up dog breeding. At one time, we had 13 Labradors and seven Pomeranians in the backyard. Albany proved to be an ideal place for our children to grow up and for Terry to master the music ministry.

ತಾತಾತಾ

"Any calls for me today?" Terry called over the joyful raucous noise of our three teenagers one summer day during lunch.

"Just one. Some church in Memphis called."

"Again?" Terry perked up fairly quickly.

"Yes, do you know who they are?"

Fearless Forgiveness

"Not really, but this is the third time they've called."

"Hmm, third time's a charm," I mused. "Do you think we need to go for a visit?"

"Memphis is a long way away. And we still have those four dogs. We would definitely need to talk to the children about it. The church is quite a bit larger as well — about 2,000."

I smiled. "It would be an adventure, Terry."

"It sure would, honey. It sure would."

Terry and I asked one of the church members to supervise the children, and we flew to Memphis. About the third day, Terry and I looked at each other and knew we were meant to move there. So we sold the house and packed up our three teenagers, the dogs and our belongings and headed east to Memphis. We found a brick ranch home with a built-in swimming pool (which was wonderful in the heat of summer) and enrolled the children in junior high. Terry got to work on the choir, and I became the music teacher for the church's Christian elementary school. With my teaching duties and being a mom to three teens, I did not have the time to start another hand bell choir, but Terry and I did implement an indoor version of the Independence Day musical. We even had indoor-friendly fireworks!

Soon after arriving, Terry began teaching a Sunday school class before church. The class quickly grew to about 150 people, and Terry seriously considered becoming a pastor. He decided to resign as the Minister of Music. When he went to the lead pastor to tell him the news, the

Voices from the Valley

lead pastor decided to make Terry an executive pastor with preaching and teaching duties.

☙☙☙

"Why don't you apply to work at Northwest Airlines with me, Janelle?" a friend asked me. "It would be the perfect job for you — it's part-time, and family members of employees can fly anywhere in the United States for only $10."

"Just $10? That would really help us get the kids out to California for a visit with their grandparents."

"Yes, and get this: If you work in the World Club, you don't have to travel. You can stay at the airport," she said.

"You make this sound like a fantastic opportunity. I will look into it."

Everything my friend said checked out, and I began work with Northwest Airlines in 2000 at its World Club. With the airport just 20 minutes away, and our children all over the age of 15, airline travel became a common mode of transportation for our family. Unfortunately, airlines suffered in the wake of 9/11, and I was let go in 2003. However, by then, Terry was considering starting a church of his own.

☙☙☙

"Where do you think our next move will be?" I asked him one day. "Jennifer is getting ready for college, and she would like to attend school someplace in our vicinity."

Fearless Forgiveness

"To be honest, Janelle, I don't know. It was so clear with Oakland and Albany and Memphis. Things fell into place, and God provided for our family. But this time, I'm not getting anything. The interviews went well in Arkansas, and I really enjoyed the staff in Minnesota, but something's missing."

"Well, we certainly don't want to move until we have that clarity. Don't worry about it, love. Jennifer should really go to the school she likes instead of choosing one based solely on geography."

Terry smiled and took my hand. "It's all part of this great adventure we've been on since we started believing in God and found each other."

☞☞☞

Eventually, Jennifer chose a school in Missouri, and Terry and I chose a church in Hood River, Oregon, with 64 people attending. God provided the means for construction of a new building, and we changed the name of the church to River of Life Assembly.

To pay for health insurance, I found work first as a bank vault teller, then as office manager for two brothers who ran a fruit orchard and, eventually, as a technician for a local pharmacy.

In a small church, you tend to do a little bit of everything, so Terry leads the music team and preaches, and I play the piano. At first, our children were very disappointed that there was only one other teenager at church, but the youth program has since grown to more than 30 teens. The congregation has grown to about 200 people. Terry says he likes it that way — when the church is big, he can only invest in relationships with the choir and orchestra. However, with a church this size, Terry feels as though he can invest in everyone. We say it's been our greatest and favorite challenge yet!

❧❧❧

"Oh, my goodness! I can't believe how much Jennifer looks like you in that photo," Terry exclaimed as we pored over pictures from our daughter's wedding one uncharacteristically quiet evening.

"I know. Mom would have loved to see her walk down the aisle … and look at our Jeremy! Isn't he handsome like his father? Can you believe he designed the t-shirts and workbooks for the children's camp this year?"

"I know — it feels like yesterday that he was a kid at camp. And now he's a senior at Oregon State."

"And there's Jamie. She looks dashing in her bridesmaid's dress. She's really come into her own, hasn't she?"

"Yes, yes, indeed. It's exciting to see our children face the challenges of life head-on and persevere, isn't it? That's when their faith truly shines — in adversity. Each one of them has had his or her own challenges, and each one has relied on God for help and support through it." Terry looked at me. "Like their mother."

Fearless Forgiveness

"And their father," I added. "The Lord is our light and our salvation. Who do we have to fear?"

Conclusion

My heart is full. When I became a pastor, my desire was to change the world. My hope was to see people encouraged and the hurting filled with hope. As I read this book, I saw that passion being fulfilled. However, at River of Life Assembly, rather than being content with our past victories, we are spurred to believe that many more can occur.

Every time we see another changed life, it increases our awareness that God really loves people, and he is actively seeking to change lives. Think about it: How did you get this book? We believe you read this book because God brought it to you seeking to reveal his love to you. Whether you're a man or a woman, a logger or a waitress, blue collar or no collar, a parent or a student, we believe God came to save you. He came to save us. He came to save them. He came to save all of us from the hellish pain we've wallowed in and offer real joy and the opportunity to share in real life that will last forever through faith in Jesus Christ.

Do you have honest questions that such radical change is possible? It seems too good to be true, doesn't it? Each of us at River of Life Assembly warmly invites you to come and check out our church family. Freely ask questions, examine our statements, see if we're "for real" and, if you choose, journey with us at whatever pace you are comfortable. You will find that we are far from perfect.

Voices from the Valley

Our scars and sometimes open wounds are still healing, but we just want you to know God is still completing the process of authentic life change in us. We still make mistakes in our journey, like everyone will. Therefore, we acknowledge our continued need for each other's forgiveness and support. We need the love of God just as much as we did the day before we believed in him.

If you are unable to be with us, yet you intuitively sense you would really like to experience such a life change, here are some basic thoughts to consider. If you choose, at the end of this conclusion, you can pray the suggested prayer. If your prayer genuinely comes from your heart, you will experience the beginning stages of authentic life change, similar to those you have read about.

How does this change occur?

Recognize that what you're doing isn't working. Accept the fact that Jesus desires to forgive you for your bad decisions and selfish motives. Realize that without this forgiveness, you will continue a life separated from God and his amazing love. In the Bible, the book of Romans, chapter 6, verse 23 reads, "The result of sin (seeking our way rather than God's way) is death, but the gift that God freely gives is everlasting life found in Jesus Christ."

Believe in your heart that God passionately loves you and wants to give you a new heart. Ezekiel 11:19 reads, "I will give them singleness of heart and put a new spirit within them. I will take away their stony, stubborn heart and give them a tender, responsive heart" (NLT).

Conclusion

Believe in your heart that "if you confess with your mouth that Jesus is Lord and believe in your heart that God raised him from the dead, you will be saved" (Romans 10:9 NLT).

Believe in your heart that because Jesus paid for your failure and wrong motives, and because you asked him to forgive you, he has filled your new heart with his life in such a way that he transforms you from the inside out. Second Corinthians 5:17 reads, "When someone becomes a Christian, he becomes a brand new person inside. He is not the same anymore. A new life has begun!"

Why not pray now?

Lord Jesus, if I've learned one thing in my journey, it's that you are God and I am not. My choices have not resulted in the happiness I hoped they would bring. Not only have I experienced pain, I've also caused it. I know I am separated from you, but I want that to change. I am sorry for the choices I've made that have hurt myself, others and denied you. I believe your death paid for my sins, and you are now alive to change me from the inside out. Would you please do that now? I ask you to come and live in me so that I can sense you are here with me. Thank you for hearing and changing me. Now please help me know when you are talking to me, so I can cooperate with your efforts to change me. Amen.

Voices from the Valley

The Hood River Valley's unfolding story of God's love is still being written ... and your name is in it.

I hope to see you this Sunday!

Terrell Abbott, Pastor
River of Life Assembly
Hood River, Oregon

We would love for you to join us at River of Life Assembly!

We meet Sunday mornings at 10:30 a.m. at 979 Tucker Road, Hood River, Oregon 97031.

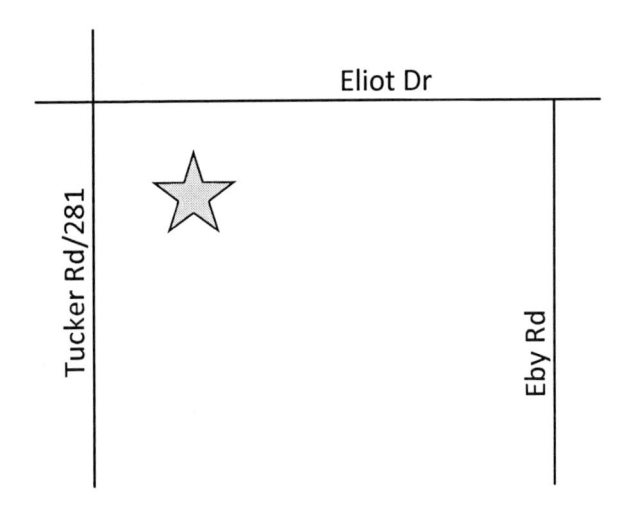

Please call us at 541.386.3656 for directions, or contact us at www.river-of-life-assembly.org.

For more information on reaching your city with stories from your church, please contact Good Catch Publishing at
www.goodcatchpublishing.com

Good Catch Publishing

Did one of these stories touch you? Did one of these real people move you to tears? Tell us (and them) about it on our reader blog at
www.goodcatchpublishing.blogspot.com.